ACCLAIM FOR TEETERING ON DISASTER

2009 San Diego Book Awards Winner

Laura Delaney of Rediscovered Book Shop, Boise, ID says "Michaela Renee is friendly, personable and all around lovely."

Pamela Mahoney Tsigdinos, Author of Silent Sorority included it in her Amazon Listmania as one of the "eclectic mix of memoirs that take a look into the unpredictable and absurd ways of life written by women with a sense of humor."

Third Place Books says, "Teetering on Disaster is a funny and poignant autobiographical novel, which tells how she fought for her American Dream through the Sierra Nevada's and beyond."

Teetering on Disaster

A Memoir

Michaela Renee

Teetering on Disaster
A Memoir

ISBN 978-0-578-43080-5

Edited by KiaKiali

References
All songs/song titles referenced are the sole copyright of their respective artists.
http://www.data.scec.org/chrono_index/northreq.html
Non Fiction | Autobiography Humor | General

For Mom, Dad & the boys…I hug you, I kiss you, sweet dreams, see you in the morning, I love you with it, goodnight…don't let the bed bugs bite!

TEETERING ON DISASTER

CONTENTS

PART I

HAPPINESS = LOVE + 3,200 SQ FT MINUS 3,000 SQ FT

THE IRRIGATION DITCH

All you really need to know is, sub-40-degree-irrigation-ditch water, goosebumps and a disposable blue razor don't play well together, period. The first time I shaved my legs I was fifteen years old, squatting on the edge of a riverbank wearing a pair of jean cutoffs, without any soap and using a ten cent disposable razor I borrowed from my dad. This was not by preference, but because it was the only running water I had access to. To some, this little episode could be deemed poetic, an idealistic event granted only to those who have had the pleasure of growing up in the Pacific Northwest.

So let me be clear, it definitely wasn't by choice and it really isn't much of a river either, because it's only six foot wide by four foot deep, making it more like a creek. Because it's man-made, the official County term for this body of water is "irrigation ditch." It begins at the base of the Tahoe National Forest and carries snowmelt from the Sierra Nevada mountain range to my podunk little town each year.

My parents argue to this day that the few years we spent living without any electricity or running water and without a toilet to flush, did not have a profound affect on my being or my life. But let me assure you, at my adolescent age, when most girls had a Gillete Venus razor, apple smelling shave cream made with Vitamin E and warm running water, it did.

If I'd been a bit younger, like my brothers, then perhaps I would have seen the value of the way of life my parents chose for us. The quote goes something like, "You can't choose your family." Good thing too, because I'm pretty certain that given a choice between the one I was born into and the picturesque normal American family I would have opted for the latter and then I never would have become the completely nutty, naïve, intelligent, Mercedes-driving hillbilly, small town girl living in a big city that I am today.

The elements that define me began with the inheritance of a dangerous combination of genes from my Mom and Dad, and so I'm pretty sure I've been teetering on disaster since birth. But the moment which began to invent my character began the summer of 1992.

STREET OF DREAMS

Our 3,200 square foot house was in the suburbs of Sacramento. Up until the mid-80s, it had loosely been the area around the two lane highway connecting Roseville with Newcastle that everyone zipped by doing ninety miles an hour because the smell of the turkey farms was just too rancid.

As the economy boomed Sactown slowly ran out of space and construction companies, including the one my Dad owned, began ousting the turkey farms one by one. They were replaced with mini-mansions, making it a perfect little suburbia, and the new "it" place to live.

The tiny helium balloon real estate market continued to expand becoming a hot air balloon floating in the clouds. Barren fields became two million dollar subdivisions, run down farm houses became "Streets of Dreams." Sacramento's rural elite flocked to the area becoming known as Granite Bay and Granite Bay became the type of area where women got dressed up just to go to the grocery store. We lived there, in one of those mini-mansions and even our family dog, a beagle named Spencer, nicknamed Houdini, lived the life of leisure.

One evening beyond the closed large French doors of my parent's office I squinted trying to hear the debate my parents had begun. Through the intolerable music of Mario and Luigi and my two younger brothers fighting over the Nintendo controller I heard Mom and Dad whispering in a dire tone. Mom was the General Manager for our incredibly successful family construction business.

"You realize this whole mess started almost five years ago with Black Monday when the stock market collapsed." Dad began.

"Five years ago was a totally different economy than today, back then we had equity to float the loans, even if it was illusory. There's not a dime of equity in any of these properties right now. Even if we sell, we'd barely break even." Mom argued back.

"Capital gains taxes will kill us…what do you want me to do about it?" Dad asked.

"I've got three specs and two lots and no incoming cash flow. I can't rob Peter to pay Paul on these loans. We're going under. I can't even afford to feed the dog!" Mom snapped.

"I'm NOT going to claim bankruptcy." Dad pleaded.

"I'm trying to tell you; even if we sell all the properties by the time we pay the Brokers we still can't afford to pay off everyone we owe."

"We sell everything then, including this house," Dad said.

"And where do you propose we live after that? We've got three kids and we're going to be in a cardboard box!" Mom yelled.

I wasn't oblivious to what was going on, I had just finished the 7th grade and while summer had started like any other I was noticing the little things. We weren't going out for pizza after softball practice, there were no more Friday night movies and Mom and I didn't have Girl's Day with pedicures and Orange Julius any longer. The hot summer brought more news of both water and economic draught.

In light of the increasing stress and tension my parents decided to let us spend the rest of the summer with my Aunt, Uncle and cousins who lived in Pismo Beach. Life with Auntie Debra and Uncle Kurt was pretty happy go lucky and our days mostly consisted of boogie boarding, eating orange and vanilla ice cream pops, and riding bikes along the boardwalk.

Before we knew it, back-to-school commercials were interrupting our MTV music videos and it was time to go back to Granite Bay. The car ride home from Pismo Beach consists of a good five hours on Interstate 5. Mom and Dad were very quiet, almost solemn. I was sitting in the far back seat of the 8-passenger Suburban and the road trip didn't seem to end. My brothers were becoming increasingly annoying and I pleaded with them to play the "Silent Game" until we reached the driveway. They agreed on the condition I give them some of the candy I had left over.

After what felt like two days had passed, we finally pulled up to the house and parked right smack in the middle of the driveway stood 200 square feet of tan and silver metal, a 27-foot Terry trailer. Suddenly the Silent Game was over and there were five conversations going on at once.

"Cool Dad, check this thing out, when are we going camping?" Jared probed.

"Jared," Mom began as she held back the fear in her eyes and replied with the confidence only a mother can, "we're not going camping…we're actually going to live in this for awhile."

I was horrified. I wanted to get right back in the Suburban and head straight back to Pismo Beach.

Mom and Dad were savvy to the quickly declining economy, too proud and too morally adjusted to claim bankruptcy, so they sold all the properties for dirt cheap, liquidated all the assets and bailed out the construction business. They scraped together enough cash, after paying off every single debt, to purchase the trailer.

The trailer was the beginning of the end result of the final decision and if your house defines you then catch phrases like "mobile meth lab," "relive the 1970's peace love and happiness dream" and "great deal, fixer-upper for family vacations" would come to mind. But mark my words; not even Chevy Chase would have been caught dead taking this thing to Yellowstone.

Between Mom, Dad, me and the boys we could have had a small football team, so once you crammed all five of us into the twenty-seven foot trailer, there wasn't room for much else.

PISS POOR BROKE

I would have opted to run a lemonade stand rather than sell my stuff; I would have even added vodka and charged a little more for clientele over twenty-one. But that still wouldn't have changed the fact that there wasn't going to be electricity where we were going and so anything with a plug was useless anyway.

In light of the crashing economy yard sales were becoming hugely popular. A person could drive down one of the "Streets of Dreams" on any given Saturday morning and make out with a car full of goods. It was like going to the high end factory outlets. My brothers and I went through our closets and picked out two sets of clothes, one for summer and one for winter but anything we chose had to fit in one camping sized backpack. We were in charge of setting and negotiating the prices for the rest of our toys at the yard sale.

I remember when the woman showed up, she looked like trouble from afar, and she was one of the types that got dressed up to go to the grocery store. She had no control over her children and their dirty fingers were touching all of our toys. Jared watched in awe as her youngest son grabbed his Nintendo controller and started hitting the buttons really hard as if he were fighting the dragon in the final round to save the Princess.

She offered Mom five dollars for her Orange Julius blender.

"I'm asking twenty-five for that, it retails for almost one hundred," Mom stated.

"Fine, I'll give you ten, but only if you throw in the Nintendo." she replied.

Mom looked over at Jared who was shaking his head violently side to side.

"Twenty. For both," Mom said.

"Deal."

The woman hastily took twenty dollars out her pocket and thrust it in Mom's palm; as if we were lesser human's than herself, even though she was the one shopping in our life. Her son grabbed the Nintendo and jaunted off toward their luxury car.

Robert had started crying. Jared tossed Mom and me a look of despair and took Robert by the hand. "Come on, let's go play some tetherball," Jared mumbled.

"But Jared, aren't you sad?" Robert asked as Jared drug him toward the backyard.

And by the end of the weekend we had the clothes on our back and we were debt free. By selling the Suburban my parents had just enough money to buy a cheap vehicle and a small piece of land in the middle of nowhere.

We were piss poor broke.

THE TRAILER MEETS GEORGETOWN

The trailer was built the year the Eagles won top record of the year for their album <u>Hotel California</u>, 1978. Too bad that albums had since been replaced by compact discs. The rest of the world was moving forward with technology and we were moving backward. The ceiling in the trailer was barely seven feet high and it came with five wheels, four on the ground and one on the rear.

It was nearing the end of July and all five of us were piled in the vehicle Mom and Dad had just purchased, a 1984 Jeep Grand Wagoneer, for the big move up to Georgetown. In 1984 the Jeep was probably the car to have, but sometime after the movie <u>Big Foot</u> and shortly after Jeep ceased production it became less than desirable and downright un-cool. Mom always did have a knack for color coordination among other things, and I must say the white trash trailer matched the ghetto Jeep quite nicely. It was like the Bundy's meets the Huxtable's.

Dad was following directly behind my uncle who was towing the trailer with his brand new Ford F150, and behind us were another five vehicles – our official "Moving Day Posse." The crew consisted of all the extended family, grandparents, aunts, uncles and cousins.

Coming from a large family of people in the construction business meant someone was always moving. Therefore it was obligatory family policy to arrive when needed with minimal notice in your sweats at 7am to enjoy a donut and Folgers coffee while helping load the U-Haul. That said, having a tight knit family of witty conversationalists meant moving day was always filled with snide jokes, great food and lots of laughter.

There was no shortage of jokes when the "Moving Day Posse" arrived at 7am to help hitch up the house with everything we had to our name already in it. If Jeff Foxworthy had been around, he would have been muttering something like, "You know you're a redneck if…" while munching through a sprinkled covered donut. And thus the "Moving Day Posse" commenced to provide comic relief rather than brute force for the forty-five minute journey up to our three acre piece of land in the middle of the Sierra Nevada's.

So here I am, crammed in between my two younger brothers in the backseat of a hideously embarrassing vehicle with my spider monkey long legs all bent up and my knees brushing the tip of my nose because my two brothers won't stop smacking each other. Being the eldest I had been placed in this position for regulation. There was only so long I would tolerate them reaching around me playing grabseys before I'd haul off and pop them both in the head. Mom knew this and it saved her some hassle.

Don't get me wrong, on occasion it would get a little too ugly and she'd whip around and smack all three of us in one swipe, me being located directly in between the driver and passenger seats always got knocked the hardest. That hot summer day, I was fed up, confused, frustrated and nauseous from the curvy roads. I couldn't help but think that all we were missing was crazy Uncle Ned and we'd be living the Griswold Family Vacation. Except this one wasn't going to end in two weeks, and even worse I would be starting the eighth grade in a new school in less than seven weeks.

The moment I knew we were in real trouble was when after the forty-five minute journey we passed a town called "Cool." We had officially arrived in Georgetown, California, Historical Landmark Number 484. Georgetown is a small mining town which is tucked away at the base of Tahoe National Forest, in between Interstate 80 and Highway 50. The sign entering town said Georgetown had an elevation of 2,654 with a population of just over 900. I think there might have been some fine print underneath that said "including cats and dogs." There was no stop light, and there was only one four way intersection in center of town where Main Street and Highway 193 crossed. Main Street featured three bars, two hotels, a gas station, a small market, a fire department and a café, and that was about it.

Georgetown was founded August 7, 1849 and its claim to fame was the Gold Rush of 1854. Since Georgetown is perched atop two mountain ranges and surrounded by the north and middle forks of the American River the only way to get there is driving one of the incredibly curvy, scary canyon roads. Lack of easy access by car, train, plane or otherwise has kept Georgetown a remote, desolate place and limited its population growth. The town managed to maintain the original feel of the 1800's, it truly was a place where everyone knew everyone else. People still waved when they passed each other on the road. The surrounding mountains, lakes, creeks and rivers were just as gorgeous then as they were in the days before gasoline powered automobiles.

We nearly threw out the suspension in the ancient Jeep trying to pull up the driveway. When the vehicle slowed to about five miles an hour. I finally just threw open the door and shoved my little brothers out.

My Uncle had done some sixty-eight-point NASCAR driving maneuvers to get the fifth wheel backed into it's formal resting spot which was located in the far corner of the property right against the property line. I was horrified when the neighbor's cows and chickens came up to the fence to witness the violation we were dropping in the middle of the natural beauty of the land.

The smell of the madrone was like iced tea dusted with honey and the pine trees were absolutely gorgeous, it reminded me of sixth grade camp at the Redwoods, sans the banana slugs. And for a second, I stood there finding my breath in the thin mountain air, taking it all in.

Through the eerie silence of the light wind blowing through the tops of the largest Christmas trees I'd ever seen I heard Mom say that everything was as beautiful and serene as she remembered.

But we were not on a yoga retreat, and beauty would become boring quickly without electricity to watch movies, gas to cook hot food or water to shower with. In just a few short hours thoughts of my queen sized bed and seafoam green Restoration Hardware duvet cover would be replaced by the sound of a zipper on a tan sleeping bag with red flannel stuffing. The good news was that no matter how bad it got we couldn't be worse off than the Donner Party.

BIG SIS TO GUIDING LIGHT

The first evening wasn't so bad; we sat around on folding chairs, just like camping, eating take-out from the only restaurant in town that didn't have "bar" somewhere in it's name. The pizza box rested on a makeshift table, a tree stump nearly three feet in diameter. Mom bought four two-liter bottles of SunnySide Select soda because they only cost twenty-five cents a piece and I couldn't get enough of the fizzy grape flavor.

I also quickly learned that if you just drink straight out of the bottle making sure to wrap both lips around the plastic when your fingers are covered in pepperoni grease and then let some of the liquid fall back in after a large gulp, none of the adults will touch the beverage which means you get it all to yourself. Reality started to set in when around six PM the last of the family backed down the driveway and headed back to their homes in civilization.

The sun didn't set until after nine PM and so my brothers and I decided to go exploring. Within an hour we were good and lost. I'd seen on TV how to mark the trail paths with things that would help us find our way home. Unfortunately for me, I have quite a few blonde moments, and what I missed was making sure you utilized the SAME trail marker and would be able to distinguish the difference in the markers from the natural landscape. Apparently making an "X" out of pine needles will not suffice, and I quickly realized on our return that there was a lot of "X's." I started wondering if my brothers had been messing with me the entire time.

But pride got in the way, and I was not about to admit we were lost. I was tired of listening to the two little shits ask stupid questions about every single thing, you'd think they'd never been outside of the city. "Yes Jared, squirrels do come in grey not just brown." "Yes Robert, that is poison oak and it will make your butt itch." "Yes, I know where I'm going; I'm just taking us the back way."

Finally I just plopped down and stared off in the distance. I was doing this to scare them, I wanted them to know I was focused and serious, when really I was lost and had NO idea how to get us home. We were at the top of a hill staring down into a little valley, which was definitely not our valley. In the bottom of the valley was a pond and I was terrified when I realized how low the sun was. But right then the pond started glistening. It was just stunning, absolutely beautiful.

This glimpse in time is referred to as "golden hour;" it's the few minutes in each day when every thing in the entire world gets to be kissed by the lips of a greater being and turn the brightest color of gold. It could be the ugliest building in the darkest city, the most rusted run-down vehicle on the longest desert road, the most depressed oak tree sitting among a desolate land and in this moment it shines as if it's been blessed by the hands of a grand creator.

I drew strength from somewhere and jumped up and started walking, picking up speed to nearly a trot. In a matter of weeks I would become savvy enough to know exactly what the compass heading of my direction was, but in this moment I was running on pure adrenalin and instinct. My brothers loped behind trying to keep up with the length in my gait and after my little stint of silence at the top of the hill they kept their mouths shut.

It was pitch black when we hit the paved road that would lead us right to our property and even though the daytime high was around 100°, it was getting quite cold by the minute.

Finally Robert, my littlest brother, gently spoke, "Sissy, what are all of those?" He whispered because he was afraid the creatures of the night would hear him. He could be cute when he wanted to be.

But I was exhausted and didn't feel like any more science lessons for the day.

"What are you talking about, Robert?" I snapped.

"Sissy! Those!" He pointed at the sky and I didn't even bother to follow his hand with my eyes.

I was going into the eighth grade, I was twelve, which meant Robert was six. Certainly old enough to know what a star was. Didn't he learn "twinkle twinkle" when he weas like two?

"They're stars, you idiot," I replied.

Then Jared piped in. "Kayla, those can't all be stars."

Okay, okay, if Jared the wise-old soul of the group was also confused, perhaps there was some legitimacy to the question. Besides, after getting us lost and now completely frightened from all the scary sounds, the least I owed them was two seconds of my attention, so I stopped and looked up.

Then I did the stupidest thing I think I've ever done. I laid down in the middle of the road. The asphalt was still warm from the afternoon sun and sent tingles up my spine. I got the chills. The view was better than any movie I'd ever seen, including <u>ET</u> which I saw at the drive-in's the first week it came out.

My brothers followed suit and we laid there another good twenty minutes talking about the stars. I told them that many of them were in fact stars but that some were planets. I told them about the Dipper and Orion's belt, and then we talked about the one blaring thing amongst that jet black sky that had originally caught Robert's attention – the Milky Way. I couldn't help but think it looked like an expressway that would lead to something delicious, like chocolate malt ball crunch ice cream in a waffle cone from Thrifty's.

Funny now to think that for Robert to have noticed the Milky Way to begin with he must have been stumbling through those woods with his neck tilted all the way back and his jaw hanging open. Lucky for me he didn't break an ankle, and even funnier to think that in those twenty minutes that we laid on the asphalt not a single car drove by.

Until this point we'd been running the bases together, big sister and younger brothers, but I'd suddenly been thrust into assistant parent mode. And in the hours that I cared for my brothers while my parents worked two jobs, I'd stopped running the bases and started pitching the ball.

ROUGHING IT

No one can claim my parents didn't have some know-how on how to rough it.

Mother was raised in a Catholic military family, her dad was of Irish descent and worked on B-52 Bombers in the US Air Force. Her mother was a young British woman and they met and married when her Dad was stationed in England during the War. She and her three siblings were uprooted constantly (London, Kansas, Germany, Washington, Texas and the Carolina's) and eventually landed in Orangevale California, a small town outside of Sacramento.

She was the youngest in the family but she really had no claim to fame in family rank because her parents doted on the middle two. Fortunately she had landed the wit and feistiness of my British grandma and inherited the tough thick skin and loud mouth of my Irish grandpa, which meant she had no trouble holding her own amongst the pack of wolves.

Dad, on the other hand, was raised by a quiet French-Canadian father and a stubborn Polish mother in a strict Catholic household. My grandparents made the journey out to Northern California from Escanaba, Michigan when my grandpa returned from WWII, and they started a very successful construction business. But the War had changed him and he mostly found happiness in his workshop, his children, and ice cream cones on Sundays after church.

He and my grandma were nothing short of baby making machines, until something tragic happened; her fifth child, Ronnie, died within two weeks of birth. For two years my grandmother tried desperately to get pregnant again, and after numerous miscarriages she finally carried a child the full nine months and Dad was born. My grandma treated him as a blessing from God and spent every waking minute coddling him.

Dad's home was your typical Americana family household in the sixties and seventies. From this stability and predictability, Dad became a thoughtful man with a hilarious sense of humor and a carefree spirit that only the spoiled youngest child in a family of seven is granted.

Mom and Dad had always been a powerhouse of a team, and they had twelve years of marriage under their belt to show for it. But our extended family thought my parents were completely crazy to walk away from everything and start life anew, especially with three young children.

Mom only had one requirement of Dad before she bit her lip and agreed to the shenanigans, she had to remain connected to civilization to provide a sense of normalcy to complete and total chaos. Dad agreed because they had learned and perfected the art of 'give and take' and truly all was fair in love and war.

My parents were both only twenty-nine years old, but my mother's hardcore-trek-across-the-world, confront anything in your path gusto and my father's creative construction-minded laid back attitude afforded them the wherewithal to face the challenge with dignity, the courage to defend their decision to the masses and the savvy to pull through the bumps in the road of roughing it.

NORTHWESTERN ALWAYS PULLS OUT ON TIME

My brothers and I had just successfully completed our first Georgetown 'gain our bearings' expedition and traipsed up the driveway well after dark. Naturally we were immediately reprimanded by Mom and Dad for disappearing without giving them any idea of where we'd gone or when we would be home.

"Since we're in the middle of nowhere I figured the same rules didn't apply," I started.

"Since we're in the middle of nowhere the rules are more extreme, you can't just run off and not tell us where you're going." Mom snapped.

"She didn't know where she was going!" Robert defended.

"Ya, we were totally lost," Jared added.

I threw a glance to both of them that insisted they were not helping.

"Can't you just be happy that we're trying to make the best of this? At least we're trying to find something fun to do." I replied.

Mom glanced over at Dad, encouraging him to jump into the conversation, but instead she finished the debate, "We'll talk about this in the morning, right now I want all three of you, go to bed!"

My brothers and I stood still, and dumbfounded, staring at each other, when Mom finally offered further direction. "Go get the tent and set it up, and then go get the sleeping bags and go to bed!"

Was she kidding? We quickly looked over at Dad.

"You heard your mother. Go!" Dad demanded.

We wandered around for awhile trying to find the best spot for the tent and after twenty minutes of tinkering with poles and pieces of fabric we had created a masterpiece that generally looked like a tent. Once inside the tent we started a round of kick and shove and eventually the three of us fell asleep out of sheer exhaustion.

The sun rises awful early that time of year and with only the protection of the faded grey tent it was impossible to roll over and sleep. The spot we picked wasn't very good, and branches, pine needles and acorns drilled into my back all night long. My long legs were bent in half and my position looked an awful lot like the girls in the box in the magic tricks that they cut in half.

I finally decided to cut my losses and began the difficult process of sneaking out of the tent, tip-toeing around small mounds in the sleeping bags that I guessed were legs, arms, and a head here and there that belonged to my brothers. Eventually I made it to the other side, only to see them twist and turn with the tremendously loud unzipping of the door flap.

The sun was blaring that Monday morning; I rubbed my eyes and attempted to let my pupils adjust while glancing around for bears or other wildlife that might be awaiting a delicious breakfast and simultaneously shook the mass of sleeping bags off my feet. The Jeep wasn't in the driveway, so I knew Dad had left for work.

That's when I saw Mom sitting about fifteen feet away in a small folding chair with her legs tucked up close to her, she was crying.

Mom doesn't cry.

I went over and knelt in the red clay dirt in front of her and started drawing some circles with the excess pine needles around my filthy feet.

"Mom, are you ok?" I whispered.

She leaned her head back and said to some object in the sky, "He didn't deliver on his end of the deal."

What she had said was quite confusing, so I kept my eyes adjusted on the ground. What was she talking about and who was she talking to? Was I supposed to answer her statement?

Mom and I were always close, but in this moment I had no idea how to comfort her. I was born into her life at the incredibly young age of 18 and we were always more like best friends than mother and daughter. We grew up together, rocking out to John Cougar Mellencamp and teaching each other the lessons of life. But this day was different, Mom was alone, she needed me and the only thing I could do was sit and wait until she was ready to talk. She eventually did, and I just sat and listened.

We sat in the dirt for at least two hours that morning as she explained to me in very adult language what was going on, and what had happened. She told me just how bad things were and what the plan for the future was. By the time she was done, I was crying too.

I always felt that I'd stifled her dreams, even though she never gave me any reason to believe there was anything she wanted more in life than to be a mom, and I couldn't help but wonder if this was somehow my entire fault. She was so incredibly smart and I felt that by being born I'd hindered her ability to become what she wanted in life. Until this moment, I'd never had the courage to ask her.

"Why did you have me?" I asked.

She didn't hesitate, "You are the best thing that ever happened to us and I have never once regretted my decision." She told me she always wanted to be a mother and Dad just sped up the process with his crappy lesson in birth control, which went something like, "The Northwestern Train outta Escanaba always pulls out on time."

Which had never worked for my grandpa, obviously, and affected me quite greatly. To this day I don't look at trains quite the same. By the time she was done talking, I was laughing hysterically, she even went so far as to say that I shouldn't feel that bad because Robert wasn't planned either. Somehow the idea that Robert was also unplanned, did make me feel better.

About this time some character who looked an awful lot like Shaggy from ScoobyDoo showed up hollerin' as he was scampering up the driveway. "Is there some Jacks Famileee up on this PropERteee?"

We were already laughing but right about then Mom fell out of the stupid little collapsing chair and hollered back, "Yeah, sure is some JACKS up in HERE!"

The guy was like a fifth grader on the first day of school, skipping over to us with some lunch box of magic tools that he claimed was going to help install a phone line.

Next thing we see is this guy scurrying up a pine tree with the grace of an overweight domestic house cat. Within five minutes he's scooting his rear back down the tree while yelling, "Yep I think Eron gonna be good to go with dat der Tele."

He shook Mom's hand, and muttered something about her being the most beautiful woman he's seen in awhile in these parts and then he was gone.

"Sonofabitch!" Mom said, "Guess your Dad did deliver on his 'connected to civilization' promise after all."

She then stood up tall and strutted over to the trailer and plugged in the old school wired telephone. I heard her punch in the number to Dad's work and I heard her request that they patch her through to him… there was a brief silence, and all of a sudden she started singing into the phone at the top of her lungs, "GREEEEEEN Acres is the PLAAACEEEE TO BEEEEEE."

At 5am that morning I was nothing more than a young girl, just barely a teenager who was trying to come into her own, and by 8am though I was not a woman by any means, I was well on my way to skipping right over being a child.

One thing would become painfully clear in the upcoming months, regardless of my fast track to woman-hood, I would always be *their* baby girl.

DAVID & GOLIATH

Aside from the fact that we had no running water and no electricity, we had the trailer situation rigged up pretty well. On one end above the fifth wheel, three small steps led up to a very tiny bed area which you had to remain bent over to walk around in. It had a little pull curtain, so Mom and Dad made this area the 'master bedroom.' The middle of the trailer was about three feet wide and had a very small sink and stove on one side and miniature refrigerator and pantry cabinet on the other.

The far end of the trailer had an L-shaped sitting area. One side of the L was just less than six feet long and the other was about five feet long. Above the six foot side was a cabinet that folded down exposing a teeny tiny loft area that was probably intended for nothing more than storage, but created a makeshift third bed.

I, being the eldest and the tallest got the six foot side of the sitting area as my bed at night, Robert, the youngest, got the five foot side. Jared landed the penthouse loft area through no choice of his own, Robert and I are both claustrophobic and if you crawled into the loft and lay completely flat you had about eight inches from your nose to the roof of the trailer, I attempted it the first night because it offered the most privacy and woke up having what Mom called a panic attack, something she knew all too well because she'd been having a lot of them lately.

Each night we would pull the sleeping bags down from the cabinet and roll them out in our respective sleeping areas and Jared would crawl up in the loft; then each morning we would roll the bags back up and tuck them away in the cabinet creating our day time living room. We did this every day and every night for four years.

The whole first week we'd been crapping in the woods and taking bird bath's using five gallon containers of water we would refill at MarVal, the local grocery store. MarVal was about a mile and a half or walking distance away. Like it was a miniature version of a real grocery store, five aisles across and featured a produce department, meat section, deli and bakery that also doubled as the Manager's office in the far back corner.

We learned that on Sundays the manager of the market held pancake breakfast for $1.50 a person. It was held in the dirt area next to the building that was reserved for the big grocery store expansion that would be happening some day. Given that it was a hot meal, and we had no power it was the best meal we got and the highlight of our week.

But the water situation was quickly becoming quite the burden. The trailer was equipped with a tiny two foot by three foot bathroom but since we had no water on the property we had no way to utilize the built in facilities.

One morning, Dad woke me up ridiculously early before he headed out for work.

"Kayla," he said, shaking me gently, "wake up, Sis. I need to talk to you."

"Yeah Dad?" I asked, while scooting deeper into the bottom of the sleeping bag.

"Come out here for a second. I want to show you something."

"Can I see it later?"

"Nope, come on get up. I have to get to work."

Reluctantly I crawled out of the sleeping bag and followed him out of the trailer. It was still pitch black outside and he was shining the flashlight that we used in the event that we needed to go to the bathroom in the middle of the night. I followed him around the backside of the trailer.

"You see that tree?" he asked.

Squinting I saw the tree perched a top a small hill directly behind the back window to the trailer, "Yeah."

"Before you and your brothers do anything today, and I mean anything, I need you guys to get it out of the ground."

"But Dad, it's…" I was cut off.

"Kayla, do you hear me? This is really important. There are tools around the front of the trailer you'll find everything you need; I need you to do this for me okay? I'm going to be home early tonight, probably around six PM, please Sis."

I surveyed the size of the tree knowing it was going to be a complete and utter bitch to get out of the ground, and then looked over at Dad. His eyes begged for help without hassle and I agreed. I turned around and tripped my way back to the trailer, pine needles jamming into the bottom of my barefoot heels and crawled in my sleeping bag and went to bed.

Laughter startled me out of a deep sleep and I jumped up and ran out of the trailer.

"What are you two doing?!" I yelled at Jared and Robert.

"Sissy, we're building a tree house, it'll be way better than sleeping in the trailer."

They were kind of on to something...and had I not had direct orders from Dad I might have jumped on the band wagon.

"No, you aren't. Get over here, Dad needs us to do something and we have to do it before we can do anything else." I told them.

But Jared was already completely committed to his task of building a tree house and after fifteen minutes of explaining how critical it was to pull this tree out of the ground, without any understanding of the importance myself, he just looked at me with a dead stare.

There would be no changing his mind. The wheels in his head said that Dad had just given us something to do to keep us busy and he saw an opportunity to improve our living situation. Not only that but he had inherited the uncanny ability to build or fix just about anything broken -or otherwise- MacGyver style from my father. Once Jared had his mind made up it was like talking to a brick wall and I'd learned fighting him was not worth the hassle.

Robert, being the youngest, was still easily persuadable, if worse came to worse I could always threaten him and that usually did the trick.

Jared had already taken all the tools that I would need for my task that Dad had already given me dibs on, so I hassled him about how hard it was going to be to build a tree house without a hammer or a saw. Jared started crying and I felt terrible, besides a hammer wasn't going to do me much good, so I let him have the stupid tools.

Instead I went and grabbed two shovels, one for Robert and one for me and we went to work on the tree. Five hours later we had still not made near enough progress to have the project done before Dad got home, but Jared's tree house was coming along quite nicely.

He had literally drafted up plans for the entire thing in the dirt. By the time he completed it, it would have three stories a rope swing and much more. Looking at the blueprints for the Swiss Family Robinson Tree House Mansion I realized he might be able to sell it on the open real estate market for a pretty penny.

But it was getting ridiculously close to the time that Dad would be home, and I, for one, did not want my rear whooped.

Jared was perched in the tree that would contain his future playhouse staring down on Robert and I, who were still staring at the minimal headway we'd made at removing the tree. We were dripping with sweat and covered from head to toe in the red clay, even my nose couldn't escape the dirt puffs and my snot was brown.

I'd had enough. It was time to put the smack down on Jared. I had picked up a few adult words from Mom and Dad, and decided this would be the time to pull them out.

"Jared, get your ASS over here and help us with this DAMN tree right now before Dad gets home and uses the paddle!" I yelled.

Jared sat there another fifteen minutes watching Robert and I, before finally crawling down from the tree. He went around the front of the trailer muttering something. He came back with the huge piece of yellow rope that he intended to be his tree house rope swing. I yelled at him to quit jerking around and he completely ignored me.

He went over to the tree and wrapped the yellow rope tight around the base and then carried the rope back to this huge boulder. He connected the other end of the yellow rope to the boulder and hollered for Robert and I to come over. Robert and I trudged over, all other options had been exhausted.

"On the count of three push as hard as you can!" directed Jared. "1 – 2 – 3!!!"

With all three of us lined up on the back side of the boulder pushing with all our might it started to roll. Next thing I know the boulder was tumbling down the hill. We stopped shoving as it gained speed and took off without us. It rolled right past the tree and went flipping down the little drop in the land.

Next thing we hear is Jared yelling, "COWABUNGA DUDE!"

I looked up just in time to see the boulder pull the tree straight out of the ground and send it sailing down the other side of the hill.

I sat there dumbfounded and even a little ticked off wondering how many hours before Jared had solved the problem, but let Robert and I suffer for giving him attitude that morning. Bottom line, Dad was pulling up the driveway, and that little tree was dead on arrival as requested.

I HEART CLEAN UNDIES 1992

So, having no water on the property with which to bathe, cook or clean quickly presented a small problem, I mean, who knew that a wood pile filled with large madrone and pine trees might also have some poison oak leaves, and that poison oak leaves when burned literally contaminate everything, including clean clothing and more specifically, underwear.

Furthermore, who could have possibly imagined that if you wear clean panties that have been located in the path of the poison oak smoke you get a rash that even the doctors want nothing to do with? Let's be honest, while a cortisone shot is a nice tad of relief, there's really no way to even begin to describe the brutal pain and itching associated with poison oak in your crotch when you don't even have running water to bathe.

But in the weeks following the move to the small hick town Mom and Dad were too busy closing up all loose ends with Dad's construction company and working two jobs. Forget water, they needed gas to get to and from work, and we needed hotdogs and canned green beans.

Mom had one job in the city and one "on the hill" and the car situation was becoming more troublesome since both of Dad's jobs were in the city.

Dad had his Class A license and skills driving heavy machinery so he took a day job working at an engineering company driving a water truck. He also knew a thing or two about cars so on nights and weekends he'd put in a few hours at Uncle Steve's machine shop. Fortunately the owner of the engineering company realized Dad was skilled beyond the position and promoted him to foreman, which meant he got keys to a company truck.

The water truck job turned out to be a complete blessing because it gave Dad the means to rectify our crappy no-water situation.

One evening Dad came home and the company truck was loaded with two huge blue fifty-five gallon water drums made out of some sturdy plastic material, plus five-5 gallon water transfer containers, a large green hose and some pipe scraps.

He immediately recruited the boys to help him build an elevated stand to hold the water drums where the little old pine tree on the hill used to be. Mom and I went to work on the garden hose; our goal was to turn it into a sophisticated siphon water delivery system.

After fussing, measuring and cutting the hose and the pipes to the perfect fit Mom opened up the can of pipe glue.

I love pipe glue. There's just something about that smelly purple glue that comes in a metal can with a little sponge applicator that looks like the puff ball on the back of the hop socks in the 50's that takes me back.

As a little girl Mom was always hauling me out to Dad's job sites in my Osh Kosh Bigosh overalls and I'd run around wreaking havoc with the construction scraps. It was always my favorite when the plumbing pipes were delivered. If I hung close to the sawhorse, they'd toss odd sized black and white pipe scraps, and on a good day there was even extra

J-fitting lying around which meant I could go get the pipe glue, dunk the little sponge applicator and swirl it around the pipes to connect the scraps together. Most kids remember their parent's cologne or aftershave, I remember pipe glue.

This particular evening the smell of that pipe glue meant we would no longer take bird baths using water jugs from the grocery store.

It was a team effort to get the fifty-five gallon drums from the truck up the hill, but within a matter of hours we had our own personal water tower and a method to get water to the trailer. The outstanding question was whether or not the delivery system would actually work.

Dad was stationed outside near the drums and Mom was inside the trailer extending her reach to the kitchen sink, bathroom sink and shower without even moving a toe. The boys and I sat around in some folding lawn chairs outside the trailer and I couldn't help but think it would be awesome if we could take the spray cans of orange paint Dad had and tag the drums with something wicked schweet like "I HEART Clean Underwear forever, 1992."

Dad opened up the valve and yelled, "Got anything?"

"No Babe, there's nothing!" Mom replied sweetly but loudly.

Sure, of course not. That would be too good to be true. After a few minutes of back and forth with the same question, the dagger throwing began.

Questions became statements, like "This damn thing is a dried up piece of shit."

"Where'd you find this anyway?" and the response, "Well maybe if you knew how to glue together a few pipes," and "WELL MAYBE IF YOU WEREN'T TRYING TO BE THE BOSS ALL THE TIME!"

The boys and I knew better than to interject so we just sat back and waited, figuring at some point something had to give. Fortunately for us and the sleeping wildlife it did, suddenly something started gurgling and we heard Mom yell "Punkin! We've got water!"

That was all it took because within seconds all five of us were quarterback-sack dog piled in the kitchen/hallway/pantry staring into the miniscule bathroom at the shower as if it were the holding tank for a rabid zoo animal.

Mom started to explain that it would take Dad a few days to fill up the entire drum so tonight we only had twenty-five gallons, but either way we wouldn't be able to shower like we used to in the "real" house.

Not like the "REAL" house? Was there something else besides the fact that I would have to crouch down in a 1x1 area with a shower head that looks more like the spray nozzle on a garden hose and that I could technically be sitting on the toilet while showering at the same time? Did she mean besides that?

And then she went into detail, evidently we would need to turn on the water and rinse down quickly and then shut the water off to soap up and turn the water back on to rinse the soap off. Then she demonstrated how to turn on and off the shower head to conserve water. Whatever, it would be the first semi-shower I'd had in over a week and I didn't care. Jared went first that night, I was second and Robert was last.

I went into the bathroom and shut the door. It was my first fifteen minutes of privacy. As I turned on the water to rinse, brown dirt ran off my body and created a swirling puddle around my feet. Using the soap was more like smearing clay because there just wasn't enough water to lather. I pretty much gave up trying to get the shampoo out of my hair knowing there were three more people behind me waiting for the remaining few gallons of water. For the first time since that day with Mom I cried.

The tears were good because I learned two valuable lessons. 1. You can cry as much as you want in the shower because no can see you and 2. No matter how little water there is, it always washes away the tears.

After my first pathetic attempt at a shower I still felt remarkably clean that night and I wanted nothing more than a clean night shirt – poison oak free - to sleep in. Mom had just taken Dad's work shirts to the laundromat and he willingly loaned me one of the super sized bright orange Caltrans-esq t-shirts with stained armpits because Dad spent all day working hard in the blistering sun.

I crawled into the bottom of the sleeping bag and laid there thinking that whoever created pipe glue was incredibly brilliant when Robert tapped me.

"Sissy, I have to go to the bathroom."

"So GO." I said.

"But I'm too afraid, will you come with me?"

Finally we had water, but we were still peeing in the woods.

WEE CHATEAU

The water system delivered enough water to the trailer that we could take mini showers, rinse off some dishes, and wash our hands. We did not however have a septic system or enough water to flush the toilet.

Therefore, the toilet in the bathroom was null and void. Literally duct taped shut by Dad with the warning, "If any of you tries to crap in this toilet, you're cleaning it up. Mark my words it won't be pretty."

Dad is 6'2, 220lbs, what he says, goes. Especially when there's duct tape involved.

So each time any of us had to go to the bathroom we had to grab the TP and hike out into the woods and cop a squat hoping we weren't hovering over poison oak. Which, in broad daylight did not present a problem, but when armed with only a Maglight and Tevas after dark was quite challenging, especially when it was chilly.

For Mom and Dad, Jared and I the frustration ended there. I for one was gaining some pretty strong thigh muscles and the trembling leg quake was becoming less and less with each "number two." But unfortunately for Robert, the bathroom break became an activity that was nothing short of petrifying.

At the very young age of four when we moved up to the hill, Robert was already twice the height and width of everyone his age and even though he was the youngest he towered over Jared. This meant Jared put forth a constant effort to establish his rank and dominance over Robert in other ways such as instilling fear and terror.

Robert was constantly harassed. Of course by the time Robert would hit high school as a freshmen, Jared, a junior, finally saw the benefit of a brother on the varsity football team that could literally take out anyone in his path, defending Mom's honor, my honor, and even Jared's girlfriend's honor simply by asking someone, "Would you like a piece of me, my fist says you might?"

But before high school would be years of brotherly love aka torment that would ultimately create a lifelong bond between the two of them.

Jared, ever the explorer, had drug Robert along on a "bear hunt" earlier that day and later that afternoon when Dad got home I heard Jared explaining in great detail the "tracks" he had seen, and the subsequent "traps" he'd set to catch these wild, crazy, people-eating animals. I sat and watched as Robert's eyes got larger and larger.

Later that night the three of us were getting ready for bed, doing our sleeping bag preparation and Robert says, "Jared, those bears won't hurt us right, I mean, they can't come into the trailer can they?"

Jared went onto explain that the bears probably could break into the trailer, but he had set up traps to catch the bears, but that the mountain lions were a little more wiley and might be able to get past the traps, but that would be okay because he had other plans to snare the mountain lions if they came close.

I saw Robert's tender mind process this concept and repeat, "Okay, but they can't get *US* right?"

About that time I chimed in and told Robert that we would all be here to protect him and that they'd get me first anyways because I was closest to the door.

This seemed to be enough to calm him but he wouldn't go to sleep, he tossed and turned for sometime.

This nightly ritual went on for a good three or four days and finally on about the fourth night Robert woke me up around two AM.

"Sissy?" Robert whispered.

"What Robert?" I replied.

"Sissy, I have to go potty really bad."

"So go."

"I can't."

"Why?"

"Because the mountain lions will eat me, Jared said they can get through the traps."

Thud. My heart dropped.

"Robert, there's no mountain lions." I reassured him, "Jared made the whole story up, everyone knows those are dog tracks."

"NUH UH KAYLA, those ones are coyotes. There's no dogs!!" Jared yells down from the slumber loft.

"SHUT IT, Jared!" I yelled with exasperation quickly growing weary of the week-long taboggle over whether or not there were bears.

"But SISSY, we SAW the tracks!"

Finally I cave, "Okay Robert, I'll take you, but just this one time, then you have to go on your own."

I slipped on the Tevas that remained stationed by the front door of the trailer and grabbed the MagLight, Robert had a death grip around my hand and we headed out a reasonable distance from the trailer. He kept wanting to stop, but I knew we needed to get a little further or it would just be straight unsanitary.

So Robert's standing there, white butt sticking out of his pj's staring at the tree in front of him and he's literally taking forever. I totally get it if you're a girl, there's the squat, keeping the pants out of the way of the dribble and the subsequent leg tremble, but c'mon, boys have it easy, unzip and pee already.

After a minute I start prodding in a night whisper voice, "Robert *WHAT'S* the problem?"

"It burns so bad, I can't really go."

That's when I realized something wasn't right. I told him to zip up and we went back in and woke up Mom. The next morning Robert was whisked away to the doctor in town. The poor little guy had been holding his pee. Since he first heard the story about the wild animals and he'd held it and developed a very bad bladder infection.

When Mom told us about it, she scolded Jared, threatening him if he mentioned another thing about the wild animals. I was told that I would be Robert's late night bathroom escort as long as he needed one; in other words, until the trailer-toilet situation was rectified.

Outlook was bleak and his potty breaks started really cutting into my beauty rest. That's when I got savvy. If that little shit even THOUGHT about drinking anything with dinner I snatched it out of his hands. No liquids after five PM!

We went on dealing with the nature's toilet situation for a good three weeks until one evening over a dinner of mac and cheese with hotdogs and green beans cooked on the Bunsen burner my parents made an announcement.

We would no longer be crapping in the woods! Hallelujah! Now if we could just get some electricity we'd be living like normal well adjusted individuals!

Not quite.

Mom and Dad went on to explain "it" would be "arriving" the next day. Arriving? Pardon? Last time I checked, toilets only "arrived" if they were "portable."

The next morning we all waited patiently for the toilet arrival. To this day I laugh hysterically at the memory of the semi truck trailer backing up the driveway to deliver the dirt brown, brand new, never been used – state of the art – name brand "Wee Chateau," which quite literally translated means "Wee Castle."

AKA "We shit in a porta-potty."

My jaw dropped. Way to go Dad!

Most people cringe at the concept of using a porta-potty in a dire situation just to go "number one" at the end of a six-hour long tailgate party. We, on the other hand, were jumping up and down at having a hard plastic seat underneath our tooshes to rest while taking a leisurely bowel movement.

The first announcement Mom made as she opened the door to the Wee Chateau was that the urinal would be the magazine holder, and she tossed some two-year-old "Better Homes and Gardens" mags (freaking comical, I know) and a half finished crossword with a pen in it.

Dad armed the Wee Chateau with two hanging fly traps and two rolls of toilet paper. I must say if you dared to look down at the overly chemically treated navy blue water it was quite pretty and smelled fresh…at least for the first person who got to use it.

The best part was Smelly Mel came once a week to empty it, too! This quickly became a huge fight. We'd line up, loaded up on a days worth of fiber and water, elbow shoving to be the first one to dump in the Wee Chateau when it was emptied, there was just something so empowering about that.

Our weekly dumper service man, Smelly Mel, must have gotten a kick out of making the rounds from the typical empty construction site and desolate parking lot to the little piece of land in the sticks; he probably thought we were completely nuts.

But we didn't give a crap; literally. We were moving up in the world, and, look at the bright side, at least no one had to worry about the courtesy flush.

KAYLA MISSES TOAST

To say Mom was cool is a huge understatement; she was young, hip, trendy, beautiful, athletic, funny, lovable and down to earth and she took me with her everywhere. My ears were pierced before age three, I busted my lip in softball before I'd started school and I got my first pedicure before I knew the definition of "primping."

When I was about seven, Mom was twenty-four and despite her love of sports and the outdoors she was, and still is, a shop-o-holic. One of my fondest memories was going to Sunrise Mall with Mom. After spending the afternoon trolling the stores together she would take me for Orange Julius, a scrumptious blended concoction that you could only get from the café at the Mall. It's like smoothie meets frozen yogurt, and it's to die for.

But Mom said her sister should have had the girl. As a teenager she was always more fond of running with the boys and had no interest in the color pink, playing with dolls or fingernail polish. Her sister on the other hand was a "priss," obsessed with clothing and tea-time and she delivered twin boys large enough to be linebackers.

Mom eventually got her boys, but not until after I had taught her a thing or two about the joys of raising a girly girl and until after she had instilled in me a love of football and the color blue.

The year before we moved to Georgetown the "Top Secret Recipes" book came out. Mom could hardly contain her excitement when she saw that they had the recipe for the Orange Julius. The first thing she did was run out to buy a state of the art blender that could do the ingredients justice, and the second thing we did was have a Girl's Night – movies and homemade Orange Julius, as many as we could suck down.

It became a monthly tradition and pretty soon my Aunts and Mom's friends were coming over, too. One night we had the blender purring up large quantities the top secret frothy invention when Petula Clark came on the radio.

All of us girls were screaming at the top of our lungs, "Forget all your worries, forget all your cares and go downtown! Where living is easy, DOWNTOWN!"

It's a night that will forever be seared into my mind as one of my favorite memories of all time, two months later we moved, and the Orange Julius nights stopped.

Pacific Gas & Electric wanted a hefty price to pull electricity to the property, and honestly we couldn't have afforded the monthly bill anyway. The basic math on this equates to the simple fact that we would be living without power for a long time.

There are certain modern-day necessities that require power; lights to read a book before bed, an alarm clock to wake you up, television to catch the local news and a radio to escape the daily humdrum of life and drown out the white noise in your head with music.

Then there are amenities that you don't really need but when living without you find yourself asking "why me?"

One night in mid-Fall, my brothers and I were sitting outside taking full advantage of the few remaining hours of daylight when Jared popped the question.

"Kayla?"

"Yeah, Jared?"

"What do you miss the most?"

I knew my answer before he finished the question, but I was curious to hear his. "I dunno Jared, that's really tough. What's yours?"

"Nintendo."

Everyone's "why me" was different and I chuckled recollecting when my grandparents bought us our first Nintendo for Valentine's Day and realized life without Mario and Luigi wasn't that bad.

"Stop laughing, Kayla. What's yours?"

"Toast and Orange Julius," I shared. "Remember Nanny's tomato tree? And how we'd go to the garden and pick the ripe ones and eat them with salt, and then the next morning we'd slice them up and have tomato on sourdough toast for breakfast?"

Both the boy's eyes glistened as they nodded in agreement. Man, I missed toast.

A few nights later we were sitting around the fire playing cards with Dad when Mom pulled up the driveway.

Her job at Papa's Pizzeria, the local pizza joint, was proving to be quite beneficial for our social calendar. She's a chatterbox and a social butterfly and the folk in town immediately took a liking to Mom. Something about that blonde hair, blue eyes and ginormous laugh was contagious in the small town.

Not to mention anyone who isn't third generation George-tonian, married to so and so's cousin who used to be married to so and so before "the accident" and has a mouth full of pearly whites is bound to stand out.

The Jeep was barely in park when she jumped out and immediately started telling Dad about some of the "regulars." Her description afforded a visual of a group of toothless old timers, who arrived before the ass-crack of dawn and continued to nurse a bottomless cup of motor oil served in a beige diner mug until well into the mid day lunch rush. But the bottom line was the Mr. Haney look-alikes were incredibly generous with the tip on a single cup of coffee.

Dad is no dummy and gave her a "yeah, I bet they tip well" glance when Jared piped in.

"Hey Mom, Kayla misses toast. Do you have enough tips to bring home some toast?"

Dad flashed me a look of slight disappointment.

"What?" I begged. "Seriously Dad, I miss toast with tomato, you know like we used to have."

"C'mon are you kidding me Sis?" he replied. Then he got up and walked into the trailer and returned with a bag of knock off Wonderbread and tongs.

He knelt down over the fire slowly crisping a boring single white slice of bread to char-grilled perfection. My brothers and I were amazed and laughing hysterically. It was like Dad was Jesus and just turned the water into wine.

"Hey Babe!" Dad yelled to Mom while joining us in laughter.

"Yeah?"

"Did the "regulars" tell you that the toothbrush was invented in Georgetown?" he asked.

My brothers and I were flipping our heads side to side to witness the dialogue between the two of them. We were flabbergasted at Dad's incredible knowledge when he tossed the toast in the air, sent it my way and finished his sentence.

"Yep, because if it had been invented anywhere else… they would have called it the teethbrush."

It would be many years before I would enjoy another Orange Julius, but the bright side was, I had all my teeth and I knew how to make toast.

BUDDY & THE BALOGNA

We'd been living on the hill for over six months and we still didn't have electricity. At this rate I was pretty convinced Jared's tree house was going to have power before the trailer and called dibs on the spare bedroom which in my opinion was going to have a better view than the master anyway.

School had begun and we'd immediately started making friends in our classes and in our neighborhood. And by "in our neighborhood" I mean it was open season on any house within a ten mile radius that didn't look like it harbored Charles Manson as the landlord. Extra bonus if there were kids our age that rode the school bus, which made a stop about a mile and a half down the road from our property.

We fell into a pretty standard routine. On weekends I would write in my journal, do chores and babysit my brothers, while Mom and Dad worked their second jobs in the city.

Jared, who was continually maturing into a little spitting image of my father, had learned he could coerce his friends into assisting with the construction on the tree house with a small promise of profits on the final development. So each weekend I'd see some group of filthy, snot-nosed kids with dirty feet and fingernails come traipsing up the driveway with their construction bags on.

Their construction bags consisted of whatever extra tools they had found lying around their own homes; amongst them they had enough to make the Craftsman section of the Sears catalog look weak and lacking. Robert's friends, on the other hand, were too young to be allowed to go romping around the neighborhood unattended, so he had to resort to following Jared and Jared's buddies around.

While babysitting my brothers and their friends too, was a complete pain, my luck had begun to change. I guess some of Jared's friends had told their older brothers that Jared had a blonde haired, green eyed older sister because before I knew it, it wasn't just scrawny kids showing up in the driveway to build the tree house.

I'll never forget that Sunday morning. It was surprisingly quiet. I woke up and the boys were gone. There was no hammering noise coming from the tree house and all of a sudden I heard a pounding on the trailer door. I slipped out of the sleeping bag, still trying to figure out where the boys had gone, and incredibly nervous that they'd gotten into trouble.

When I opened the door someone thrust at me wearing a Halloween mask. I screamed Jamie Lee Curtis style at the top of my lungs and ripped the mask off their face to expose them.

At that moment the boy tumbled backwards and yelled, "Holy shit Jughead! Your sister doesn't play around!"

As I stood there in my pj's (orange construction shirt of Dad's and boxer shorts) staring at the lanky, blonde haired, blue-eyed older brother of one of Jared's friends I realized that they had started using Jared's childhood nickname. All of Jared's friends were on the ground laughing and Jared was too, the jerk.

Even though my heart was pounding from having just been punked, it started skipping as I glanced up from the immediate interest I had taken in my feet. My God.

Who was this potty mouthed, with the shit-ass grin on his face, dusty blonde hair falling over his forehead in a tousled mess, t-shirt, cut offs and hiking boots, perched in a cocky stance, absolutely adorable guy standing in front of me?

In an effort to evade staring, I scanned the property for Robert, when I didn't find him, I shoved by "PottyMouth" who was still blocking the trailer door. I headed down the driveway and found Robert down near the burn pile.

"Whatcha doin?" I hollered from about ten feet away.

"Nothing, Sissy." Robert yelled back.

"Yeah right!" I continued.

As I approached I saw what had gathered his interest and about crapped my pants for the second time that morning. It was a reddish-brown fluffy mutt with huge brown eyes, surrounded by black eyeliner, and dangly soft ears.

Robert was crouched down feeding it something.

"What in God's name are you doing? IT COULD HAVE RABIES!" I screamed at him.

"Shhhh, its ok," Robert whispered.

As I approached, the dog cautiously came forward, tail between his legs and I bent down with my hand out.

"I named him Buddy," Robert offered.

I looked up to see my little brother's face, filled with excitement that finally Jared wasn't the only one with friends and I melted.

"Buddy...c'me here Buddy," I extended.

Robert sighed a bit of relief and I started asking him questions to learn more about his new furry friend. Turns out that Buddy had been coming around for about two weeks.

He'd leave for hours every day, but come back about the time Robert got home from school. Robert had made him a little den down by the burn pile. Oh, and Robert had been sneaking him bologna because he loved him.

Well, no-freaking-wonder the dog was coming back every day. I had quite the dilemma on my hands, and I really wasn't sure what to do. Before we'd moved to Georgetown my parents had given away Spencer and it had about killed all of us.

They'd gathered us up in the living room. They had Spencer, Spencer's food bowls, his bed, and his toys and they told us they just couldn't afford to feed him, that he would be much better off with some friends of ours.

We all gave him final kisses and hugs and watched as my parents loaded him up in the car for the last time. We were devastated when my parents took off down the driveway. Robert had found one of Spencer's tennis balls in the yard and started crying, asking me if maybe we could still go play with him.

So here I am staring at my brother, shaking my head trying to figure out what to do. When Robert posed a question. "Kayla, will you please not tell Mom and Dad?"

I looked up at my brother and I looked over at Buddy who had plopped down in a circle at Robert's feet. I looked back over at Robert and nodded. He had my word.

Two more weeks of sneaking Buddy bologna had gone by. It was a Saturday afternoon and Mom had done something really special, she'd gotten an extra $20 in tips that week so she brought home Nathan's hotdogs, the extra large buns, potato salad and real brand name Coke. We were ecstatic. She had gotten off work in the city early and had started the fire to cook the hotdogs. The smell was mouth watering.

Trouble was, even Buddy thought so. Next thing I see is Buddy trotting across the property headed for the makeshift grill as Robert screams, "BUDDY, NO!"

And simultaneously Mom yells, "Robert! What is that?!"

"Mom!! It's my dog!" he pleads.

"When did you get a dog?" she screams back.

"Kayla and I adopted him!" he stammered out.

Oh great.

Mom's gaze shifted over to me with a look of, "really Sis, really?"

So immediately I launch into a big long explanation and concluded with the fact that Robert said Buddy followed him home for the first time from the bus stop. The bus stop was located in the parking lot of MarVal.

A light bulb went off in Mom's head. Hotdog in hand she runs over to the Jeep with dumb, stupid Buddy galloping happily behind her. She hollers at him to get in, and of course, like a kid promised candy by a guy in a white van, the dog hopped right in.

Robert and I leapt through the windows of the Jeep Dukes of Hazzard style after Buddy as Mom threw the Jeep in reverse.

The whole time I'm trying to get right side up in my seat and Robert is pleading with Mom, she's trying to figure out how this dog had been surviving on bologna for four weeks and figures he's probably been going home to his 'real' family during the hours of the day he was missing. Made sense that he'd followed Robert home from the bus stop. He'd probably jumped out of someone's truck at MarVal. But Robert knew better - and told her such.

Mom whips the Jeep into the MarVal parking lot, tosses the hotdog out and the dog jumped out after it, then she squealed out of the lot. We were headed full speed back to the property when all of a sudden Robert shrills from the backseat, "Mom! Buddy is following us!"

Mom gunned it and I swear I've never seen a dog run so fast and hard in my life. My mouth absolutely dropped. Mom's did too, but she shifted gears and kept on going. The dog had just about caught up to the tail of the vehicle too when Mom rounded the corner. As soon as Buddy was outta sight Robert started wailing at the top of his lungs.

The sound was not only obnoxious but it was heart wrenching. The poor kid had nothing but this ridiculously faithful dog which had stuck around and survived on nothing more than a few bites of bologna.

The next thing I remember is Mom popping the clutch and spinning it around in the middle of the road and accelerating for the grocery store. Robert and I were thrust to the back of our seats with the seatbelts locking up tight against our chest. What the heck was going on? All I knew was that I'd had a lot of Coke and I was about to pee my pants, all this crazy driving was NOT helping the situation.

When she caught up to Buddy he was standing on the road side panting and looking completely confused. Robert immediately hopped out and threw his arms around the dog. Mom looked at them and then hollered for both of them to get back in the Jeep.

She then paused, half parked-half not, on the side of the road. She looked at me and she looked at Robert and then she calmly continued onto towards the grocery store.

She pulled into a parking spot and pulled out her wallet. She clutched at her head for a minute as she glanced in the bottom of it. I still wasn't sure what to make of all this. I knew I'd helped sneak Buddy bologna and was therefore somehow responsible.

Mom looked at me and pulled out seven dollars in ones and emptied all the coins out of her purse. "Sis," she started.

"Yeah Mom?" I replied.

"Can you go into MarVal, find whatever the cheapest bag of dog food they have is and buy it...there's just over seven dollars here," she finished.

Mom had just handed me literally every last cent she had to her name, the remainder of her tips. As I sauntered head down into the grocery store I picked out a twenty pound white bag with blue writing, DOG FOOD $6.98, and headed toward the cashier.

As I handed the cashier the last of the money we had for the week I promised myself that the very next morning I'd start looking for a babysitting job.

BLESS US WITH YOUR PRESENTS

Georgetown doesn't have a stoplight because there's only one place where four roads cross. It doesn't have a fast food restaurant because the single gas station in town hosts Chester's Fried Chicken and maple donuts. But it does have the Georgetown Hotel (the old historic miners stomping ground), three bars with three different 'crowds' of locals, and an airport.

Says a lot in and of itself, upon arrival in Georgetown you either drink yourself into a stupor and pass out, or hop the nearest Cessna flight outta dodge.

If thoughts of grandeur and typical airport-like amenities such as a paved runway, air traffic control tower and a parking lot are coming to mind, then you better get yourself a scotch on the rocks and plan on hanging with the locals at the Miner's Club for the night.

The Georgetown Airport is perched atop one of the highest peaks in the Sierra Nevada foothills, the runway is just barely long enough for a taildragger (just ask a few people who didn't stop short enough) with a daring 2500 foot drop to the bottom of the ravine just off the edge of the strip, and it's only Visual Flight Rated (VFR), which means, if your name is JFK Jr., don't even think at attempting a landing.

Additionally, there's a group of people known as the "Friends of the Georgetown Airport" (FGA) who volunteer their time to keep the airport nice, do routine maintenance and throw annual events to welcome pilots from distance cities to the quaint little town in the mountains.

It wasn't like my parents were floating in free time; quite the contrary, but in the six months we'd lived in Georgetown they had really taken a liking to the town and the people, and had started to establish the sense of pride that goes along with living in a small community.

So naturally when the opportunity arose, they joined the ranks of Friends of the Georgetown Airport. It wasn't long before we were knee deep in airport activities and events, the members of the FGA were good people, with big hearts and they accepted us like family.

Somewhere amidst all of our activities, volunteer work and school work the holidays snuck up. Mom and Dad had started dropping hints that Christmas was going to be light this year.

Dad used the boys' new found enthusiasm for all things air travel related to explain the technical specifications on the new sled he had heard that had been developed by the elves for Santa to fly. It was much faster than the sled he'd used last year, but just wouldn't be able to carry as many toys. Dad went onto explain it was a good trade off because it meant Santa wouldn't have to miss so many kids this year and almost everyone would get presents after all.

Holiday traditions like lavish meals and decorations come with hefty price tags. My parents couldn't afford Christmas cards, let alone a Christmas tree. The whole concept of decorating the trailer in Christmas lights was out the window because we still didn't have electricity.

But Jared had heard that some families in town went out and cut down their own Christmas tree for Christmas aka FREE TREE. In years past, our trek for the family Christmas tree involved driving down to the local Home Depot and picking one out of the parking lot, so this whole "cut a tree from the forest concept" seemed like a novel idea and thus a new family tradition was born.

Our property hosted tons and tons of deciduous Christmas-like trees so Dad armed Jared and Robert with a hack saw and a handful of rules, the first was, do not accidentally remove any of your own extremities and was followed by additional rules like, do not run while carrying the hacksaw, and, if you must run- run with the blade pointed down.

A brief demonstration of how to properly pull the hacksaw through a board of wood ensued and then Mom and Dad headed up to the airport to get some last minute work done for an upcoming annual airport event.

Jared looked over at Robert and made some comments about not needing him to come along, but Robert was adamant that it was his Christmas tree, too. Thus the boys were off, facing the huge challenge of finding the Griswold-Family Christmas Tree amongst a rather large forest and bringing it back home to our humble abode.

I had just turned thirteen and was full of teenage attitude wanted no part of the Chevy Chase tree hunt.

Mom and Dad returned from the airport a few hours later. It was getting rather dark and the boys still weren't back. Dad and I were sitting around talking about the holidays and he launched into some big schpeal about the fact that family was the most important thing during the holiday season.

I think he had too much brandy in his eggnog, because if I'm being honest, he was getting a little sentimental. All of a sudden he starts blubbering on about the fact that I was going to be in high school in a few months, and it would fly by, and before we knew it I would be going away to college.

"Sis, you sure you don't want to stay here and go to college?" Dad asked.

"No way. Dad, as soon as I'm old enough, I'm skipping this podunk town." I replied.

"But what about Sierra College?"

"Nope, I'm going to a four-year."

"Well, what about CSU-Sacramento?" he continued.

"No, Dad, absolutely not. I'm going to a university with a journalism program and it won't be near here." I stated firmly.

He pondered this for a bit, and with a sad look in his eyes he asked, "Well, I mean, you'll come home for the holidays at least, right...and bless us with your presence?"

"Seriously Dad? I mean I'll come home, but I will be a starving college student, I'm not going to have any money to buy you guys presents."

And with that, Dad's expression turned from sheer depression to complete shock.

I heard Mom start cackling from the other end of the trailer. "No you idiot!" Mom yelled. "He's not saying 'presents' as in gifts, 'presence' as in come home and bless us by being here!"

We were all completely busting up, tears pouring out of our eyes when we heard Jared screaming, "I got the Christmas tree! Open the door, Robert!"

Keeping the door shut barely kept the inside of the trailer warm as the temperatures sunk below freezing and a blast of cold air welcomed us as Robert yanked open the door.

My parents eyes about popped out of their head when they witnessed the tree that Jared had delivered. Robert was bent over at the waist, huffing and puffing and half cursing under his breath and completely soaked in sweat (despite it being absolutely bitter outside.)

No joking, we stood in awe at the tree Jared had produced, it was ten-feet long, nearly a foot in diameter. It was missing half it's pine needles, one side was completely bare of branches from being drug across the forest and it was by far the most goofiest, odd shaped, scraggly tree I've ever seen in my life.

The kicker of it was, the roof of the trailer was shorter than the dang Christmas tree. So either we were going to have to re-plant it outside or Dad was going to have to come up with a better plan.

Jared was still standing there with the tippy top of the tree dangling out of his sap covered fingers, hacksaw hooked under his elbow looking for some sort of praise.

And with my hip thrust out to the side, hand perched on it modeling the perfect thirteen year old-brat pose, I smiled, thrilled I was no longer the only idiot in the family and immediately seized the opportunity to start a round of Christmas carols, beginning with the Chevy Chase Christmas Vacation theme song. "Mele Kalikimaka is the thing to say… On a bright Hawaiian Christmas Day…"

"Jared," Mom started in between her laughter, "This sure is a really nice tree. You and Robert did a great job."

Dad just stood there rubbing his chin and surveying the tree for a good three more minutes.

You had to admire the boy's tenacity. It was no small feat to hack down a tree over twice his height and drag it half way across the woods back to the house. Obviously, during the journey home, it lost a few branches, and pine needles, but hey – that only added to its character.

"Good job, Son," Dad chimed in. "I think what we're going to have to do is take off the top of the tree so that we can get it inside."

And by the time Dad got done taking off the top two feet of the tree, if there ever were a real life Charlie Brown Christmas tree, we had it.

We put the tree on the one flat table-like part of the trailer in between the "kitchen" and "Mom and Dad's room." For a whole week every time we came in and out we were forced to admire the straggly tree covered in home made ornaments and draped with lights that would never be illuminated. But if a tree ever had to lose its life to a hacksaw, this cause was worth it. Each year Christmas trees come and go, but this one will never be forgotten.

Christmas Eve finally rolled around and the boys and I were about to go to bed, with little expectations on what Santa would deliver under the tree the next morning. Just as we snuggled in we heard a loud POP POP POP and then a horrendous humming noise from outside. All three of us sat up just in time to see Mom plugging in the lights on the tree. All of a sudden our Charlie Brown Tree was lit from top to bottom.

Dad had gotten a small Christmas bonus and had used it to buy a gas powered generator. He had waited until we went to bed and he and Mom fired it up and lit up the little tree. And to the faint light of the Christmas tree we sat as a family, tears in our eyes, talking, laughing and playing cards until the generator ran out of the little bit of fuel Dad had put it in it.

Christmas morning came. Mom and Dad couldn't afford wrapping paper, so our gifts came wrapped in blankets. We didn't get much, but we each got something very special. I don't recall what the boys got, but I'll never forget what I got, a set of Jacks, a writing tablet with markers and a brand new journal.

The last present was a group gift, so each of us held an edge of the blanket and began to unwrap cassette tapes and batteries. The boys and I looked at each other confused as Dad produced the 1980's VHS video camera they'd been storing at my grandparent's house in the city. They told us we could use the camcorder to start filming our hiking excursions and making our very own documentaries.

My parents barely had a dime to their name, but they made sure we had something to open on Christmas morning and they went out of their way to make sure Christmas was as special as it could possibly be.

After opening our presents my parents said they had one more surprise for us but we needed to take a little drive. We piled in the Jeep and within a few minutes were pulling into the Georgetown Airport.

When we got to the runway I got my first glimpse of the "Christian Eagle" in all its glory. During their time volunteering my parents had become friends with a man from out of town who owned the stunt bi-plane, he was there and it was waiting for us. Dad explained that it was a special plane that could do tricks, and that the captain was going to take each of us up in it.

I climbed in to the tiny seat next to the pilot and he locked me into the five-point harness. Before I knew it we were upside down over the snow capped mountains of Lake Tahoe. We did barrel rolls and hammerheads and the whole time my stomach was in my throat. I've never smiled so big, laughed so hard and been so terrified all at once. Georgetown was stunning from the air.

I always knew there was a huge world out there for me to explore, but in this moment, all I cared about was how lucky I was to be with my family on Christmas.

Jared went next and Robert went last. After he touched down the pilot unbuckled him from the harness and he came skipping over to Dad giggling and laughing and said, "Dad, I totally get it! No wonder Santa couldn't fit more toys. There's practically no room in there!"

BBQ RIB ETIQUETTE

I'd spent Friday nights in the eighth grade on the bleachers at the high school football games watching the cute boys running around in their pads and football gear while the cheerleaders chanted on the sidelines, "First and ten! Do it again! We like It! We like It!"

I had decided that the only way to face high school was sporting Grizzly (our high school mascot) pride in the form of a gold and black cheerleading skirt, kick pants, and a vest with my name on it.

There was just one problem, Mom and Dad; didn't have enough to cover the expenses if I made the squad, and the money I was raising by working barely covered Buddy's food. So I phoned up my grandparents and presented my sponsorship case using "I'm going to fight my way out of a bogus traffic ticket" determination and pride.

To say my grandparents laughed would be kind. I was not only the oldest grandchild, but also the tallest and the only other girl is my youngest cousin Lauren. Becoming a cheerleader meant I wouldn't be bringing home any collegiate awards, or Olympic medals in basketball, volleyball, softball, soccer, tennis, golf, or any of the other sports I'd been thrust into my whole life. In other words, I would be a complete and utter disgrace to the entire family of athletes.

Eventually my family agreed to help out on one condition, that I kept a "B" average in all my classes. They had absolutely no tolerance for ignorance, naivety or stupidity, and cheerleading was not going to get in the way of my education.

Additionally, since my parents were still working two jobs each, I would still need to take care of my brothers after school, make sure their homework didn't slip and ensure that they had dinner and were put to bed every night.

I saw no choice and took the challenge. I was ecstatic when I made the team. I was quickly learning how to multi-task and prioritize a hectic schedule of holding a job, excelling in school, being a cheerleader (which was more than a full time commitment for the other girls) and raising my brothers.

There's just one problem, in a small town, football truly is life…and cheer quickly became my obsession. Besides, the mathematical equation is just flattering; boys = football, football = cheer therefore cheer = boys.

I don't think I realized that the blonde-haired, blue-eyed, cocky, lanky kid from down the street who I'd called "PottyMouth" had become a running back on the Varsity team until at least half way through the first football game. But when he came out of the locker room after the game his hair was wet, and he'd looked a lot cuter than he had a few summers back when he'd first scared the crap out of me with the Halloween mask.

I was sitting on the curb with my brothers waiting to get a ride home from one of the cheerleader's moms, when, to my chagrin, his brothers ran over to my brothers and started chatting it up.

On occasion his bratty brothers had come to the house to help Jared with the tree house which was nearly complete and looked a lot more like Home Depot- three stories, with a sophisticated pulley system to accept deliveries and housed all his various ACME inventions.

After a minute or two "PottyMouth" strutted over and my chest started pounding a little bit. All the awkward first moments ensued and I quickly directed the conversation to the game, next thing I know, he's asking me if I'd like to get a ride back with him instead.

YES I wanted a ride back with him instead! But I just wasn't sure how that would go over with my parents. After a good ten second deliberation I decided since his folks we're volunteers with Friends of the Georgetown Airport too, and our younger brothers were friends it'd be just fine.

As we walked up to his truck he threw his letterman jacket around my shoulders before opening my door. I knew right then that he was going to become a problem. A football player, with a driver's license, who lived just down the street, had just put his jacket on me! Cheer = Trouble.

It wasn't long before we were spending hours together, it was quite convenient that he had younger brothers too because he didn't mind that mine tagged along.

I was plugging away at an epic teenage novel in my journal on my newfound love interest when something really terrible happened. I brought home a C in Geometry. When I saw the grade on the report card I seriously considered tossing it in the burn pile.

Then I realized it'd be pretty difficult for my parents to implement Plato-o-Plomo strategies when you don't have any negotiation tools such as allowance. And it's incredibly difficult to punish a teenager with the peril of doing dishes or laundry when there is no running water. Not to mention the threat of scrubbing the bathroom was just a complete joke among us, since we were still using the Wee Chateau.

But the C didn't fly and there was no way I was escaping it. I was officially grounded. My punishment was harsh. I wasn't allowed to go to cheer practice until after I finished one small task.

Dad had recently managed to get an incredible deal through his job at the engineering company to lay the foundation for the house. They had framed it up, and poured the concrete the weekend before. The dump truck had showed up mid-week and offloaded a bazillion tons of gravel into what was the very beginning our future home.

Trouble was, the foundation for the house was built into a hill, and they could only dump the gravel into the deep end. Somehow the gravel had to get evenly spread across the bottom.

Task assigned. I seriously think I would have rather made fire by banging rocks together, or solve world hunger than suffer this punishment, and I'm pretty sure I popped off and told Dad so. But missing cheer practice meant I was sitting the bleachers at the game sans the uniform, which was nearly the equivalent of walking around with a big scarlet letter on your chest.

So I called varsity running back/BF/artist formerly known as "PottyMouth" to shed my tears and report my massive dilemma and he quickly came up with a solution.

He phoned Dad and asked if they could offer a hand with my punishment. Dad was impressed with his willingness to help (especially since he'd likely played a large role in my C grade to begin with) and eventually agreed to it, he even went on to promise that he'd barbecue beef ribs for dinner for everyone who showed up to help.

I'd never had BBQ ribs, but I knew they must be pretty delicious because the following Saturday morning he showed up with his brothers and half his friends with shovels in hand ready to go.

So here we were, facing down a massive challenge. Pretty soon he and I were head to head on who could shovel more gravel, which encouraged all the others to keep up. I started firing snide comments attacking his manliness, something about it being plainly obvious he wasn't a good football player because he couldn't even shove a little gravel let alone a line-backer and pretty soon his friends were following my lead.

It was hotter than hell, we'd been pushing rock for a good four hours, and we were exhausted. I sunk the shovel in especially deep and hollered at him, "What'dya got, all of five rocks on that shovel?!"

I snuck a peek to see his reaction, I'd sent him over the deep end. He started towards me as he ripped his shirt off exposing his sweat laced six-pack. He had a look in his eyes that said I was seriously busted.

In one single motion he took the shovel out of my hands and dropped it in the gravel. Using every single muscle from his sixteen-year-old stomach he threw me over his left shoulder and stormed down the driveway.

I screamed with laughter and terror, calling for my brothers to help, but instead everyone dropped their shovels and ran after us.

With half the neighborhood in tow he carried me kicking and screaming, rear end in the air the whole way down a tremendously long hill. I was still bouncing up and down on his back as he darted through the woods behind someone's house and trekked across a small valley.

Upside down and through my crossed eyes I could still make out pairs of gravel dust covered tennis shoes trailing behind us. In a matter of minutes we were headed straight for a stream of running water I was all too familiar with… the irrigation ditch.

Two seconds later I hollered out one last pathetic plea and gripped onto him for dear life as he sent us both into the glacial water together. Right then in complete shock and near hypothermia he planted a kiss on my lips, and stole my tongue too, right in front of everyone.

To my complete mortification my brothers had witnessed the whole thing and all I could hear were whoops and hollers from all the innocent bystanders. I politely asked him, at the top of my lungs, using all three parts of his full name, just who he thought he was and proceeded to jump out of the death water and stomped off for home.

Half yelling and half laughing he yelled, "You needed to be taught a lesson, Michaela Renee!" The display was quite dramatic, and if it weren't for the fact I was so pissed and had so much pride I might have spun around right then and went back for another kiss. I sorta-kinda liked it.

I started trudging up the driveway looking like a complete drowned rat. Dad and Mom were both home and had already fired up the grill for the BBQ ribs and I wanted nothing to do with the curious looks they were giving me. One fleeting glance towards the gravel pit told me I'd fulfilled my end of the bargain.

Shortly thereafter the rest of the crew appeared from the woods, laughing like hyenas. They proceeded to tell the story starting with, "And she was harassing him so bad, saying he's sucks at football…"

Mom and Dad's simultaneous perusal at my drenched tank top and jean cut offs led them to believe somehow I'd gotten what I'd deserved. The story became incredibly exaggerated and it wasn't long before everyone was laughing at my expense.

I plopped down at the far end of the picnic table away from everyone, I was frustrated and pouting. Dad threw the ribs down in the center and everyone tackled them using their dusty fingers to dig into the pile. I reached in and took one out and politely began eating mine using a knife and fork. Obviously there is proper BBQ rib eating etiquette and it does not involve a fork and knife. But, since I'd never actually had BBQ ribs I was not privy to the protocol.

Dad finally looked over at me and told me to put down the fork and pick up the damn rib and eat it. Honestly, I wasn't having much luck my way at all, so I went for it. I was surprised how tasty the little gristle on the end of the rib was and began gnawing to get every last ounce of the barbecue sauce off.

Suddenly I felt the burning heat of all their eyes on me and I paused to look up from my zealous work.

The teenage boys with all their testosterone were giddy, Mom was mortified and Dad just sat there laughing in disbelief.

For the record, it's absolutely not appropriate to grasp the rib at the base, sink the bone deep into your mouth and proceed to gnaw off the gristle and devour the delicious sauce using your tongue. Who knew?

My parents had witnessed the banter between me and the guys, and that combined with the way I ravaged the BBQ ribs meant I was going to be locked up until I was well over eighteen, never to see the light of day again - cheerleading practice was completely out of the question.

My parents rose the requirements to an "A" average after that, but it didn't matter because that was the last "C" I ever brought home. And while he wouldn't be my first love, that afternoon, in a freezing cold irrigation ditch, "PottyMouth" became my BF and the exclusive owner of my first kiss.

HAMSTERS DON'T HAVE TAILS

Dad had left for work hours before. Mom was screaming that someone had hooked up the trailer and was taking us down the driveway, Jared had just cracked his head tumbling from the small opening in the tiny loft/storage cabinet and Robert was yelling something about Effie Lynn.

I just sat there in complete shock.

The Northridge earthquake had a 6.7 magnitude and struck the Los Angeles region shortly before dawn on Monday, January 17, 1994.

The earthquake occurred on a blind thrust fault, and produced the strongest ground motions ever instrumentally recorded in an urban setting in North America. Damage was wide-spread, sections of major freeways collapsed, parking structures and office buildings collapsed, and numerous apartment buildings suffered irreparable damage.

I'm not sure much of Georgetown felt it, but Mom had nailed it. It was literally like someone backed a truck up the driveway, hitched us up and was towing us away, making sure to hit every pothole. If we'd been at Disneyland, the ride would have been called Thunder Mountain, complete with the gold rush scenery.

I don't know what the seismic hazard rating on a 1970's trailer is, but while the earthquake caused widespread damage to Southern California we faired well, our biggest travesty was that Effie Lynn was missing. At some point during the utter and complete chaos and the violent shaking and tremors Effie Lynn's cage had busted open and she had escaped.

Problem was we weren't even supposed to have Effie Lynn to begin with. Jared had come home from Mr. Babcock's class and explained to Mom that Mr. Babcock had hamsters, the class voted on who could bring a hamster home during holiday weekends to care for them, the standard stuff, food, water, etc.

Mom is definitely an animal person- the fuzzy ones- that is, and she did let us keep Buddy after all, but if they fall under the reptile or rodent category, her general philosophy is that they are filthy and belong outside. They make good sprays and traps to keep those things far away from human contact.

Jared begged, and Mom finally agreed. Especially since Jared, being the free spirit that he is, would learn a good lesson in responsibility. The deal was simple; Jared brings the hamster home on Friday, takes care of it over the extended weekend and returns it to class on Tuesday after the Martin Luther King holiday.

Mom picked Jared up a little book at the library "My First Hamster" and since all the hamsters at the school lived in the cage together, she also brought home a cheap little hamster cage with a wheel.

Jared rode home on the bus with the hamster in a box and proudly strutted up the driveway. The minute he opened the box I knew we were in trouble.

Mom came home a good three or four hours later and immediately asked to see the hamster, Jared was thrilled to show her. He escorted her over to the little cage that had been set inside the trailer on the flat part above the cabinet where the Christmas Tree had been.

Mom leaned cautiously in taking a closer look and then looked over at the "My First Hamster" book.

"Um, Jared?" Mom asked.

"Yeah Mom?" Jared replied.

"Did you notice a little difference between the picture of the hamster on the book I brought you and this creature?" she continued.

"Yep!" Jared proudly announced, "My one is grey."

"And?" Mom requested.

"And, mine is bigger!" Jared exclaimed.

"Right, and this one has a tail. Do you see that tail, Jared?"

"Yes."

"Jared, hamsters DON'T have tails like that. THIS IS A RAT."

School was closed for the extended holiday weekend and it was too late for Mom to do a thing about it. We were stuck with the rat.

Robert was quite optimistic and piped in that he thought she was cute and looked like Fievel Mousekewits from <u>An American Tale</u> and requested we call her "Effie Lynn." Mom really couldn't argue with the fact that she was in fact quite cute. The boys had been giving her little scrapings of lettuce and she would sit up on her hind legs and put perfect little rat bites in the lettuce chewing from side to side and then she would lick her claws clean and continue on.

By putting "Mousekewits" in the name, it somehow made it easier to stomach that not only were we living in a trailer, but now we had a pet rat. Plus, it was more like rat-sitting anyway, just an extended weekend, nothing more.

And for three days we had a blast playing with Effie Lynn Mousekewits.

She was incredibly trainable and loved to ride around on Robert's shoulder. The three of us became quite fond of the little rat and how she would crawl around, up your shirt sleeve and out the collar and then nibble at your ears, which tickled.

Admittedly, it was still kind of creepy having a rat around the house, and her tail was disgusting. But it was pretty incredible how she could wrap it around anything and use it as a tool, she even hung upside down!

Within twenty-four hours we were all incredibly impressed with her, and even though Mom was still on the phone to her friends insisting she never agreed he could bring home a rat, even she had taken a liking to Miss Effie Lynn.

So here it is, Monday morning, just before dawn, we're all sound asleep – sans Dad - in that stage of the morning when you are just polishing off the last of a very nice dream and suddenly the trailer is imitating a buckin' bronco. The view from the outside in would have us looking like something between the little silver ball on the pin-ball machine and kids at the fair in the bouncy machine.

When Mom finally realized that Dad wasn't pulling some prank and that we were not in fact being hooked up and hauled off to Mexico she warned us that it was an earthquake and there could be after shocks.

We had the generator and by this point we had a thirteen inch TV set up on a TV stand in the make-shift living room. Mom fired it up and tuned into the news. We stared at the mess that had become Los Angeles and wondered how we'd felt the quake so far away.

Robert and Jared could care less about the quake or the aftershocks, Effie Lynn was missing and she was due back in class first thing in the morning, tardiness didn't go over well in Mr. Babcock's class.

We spent a good three days looking for that rat to no avail and finally Mom had to have "the talk" with the boys, plus she had to explain to Mr. Babcock that there was a small problem with the durability of the cage and the drive of the little creature to escape, after all -isn't this the reason they use rats for testing? They must have some wits about them!

Robert and Jared were absolutely devastated. I tried convincing the boys that Effie Lynn was probably living the life of leisure in the great outdoors, exploring the untapped wilderness and sewing her wild oats with more available bachelor rats and wasn't dead after all.

It was nearing the end of the week and we still hadn't found her. Dad came home and shared with us that he had gotten Sunday afternoon off and was taking us somewhere special. He had a friend at work who raced Sprint cars and we were going to get to go see him race this weekend.

Dad went on to explain in detailed terms the concept of the Sprint car to the boys and pretty soon Effie Lynn was a distant memory.

We went to bed early that Saturday night, after playing Yahtzee and eating meatloaf with mashed potatoes for dinner, things were really looking up for us. The progress on the house was coming along quite nicely and the finances were stable, we were finally getting ahead, and slowly enjoying the more standard things in life, like the occasional generator/ TV night, who doesn't love a good Cosby rerun?

It was sometime around two AM, and suddenly Mom was screaming at the absolute top of her lungs. Dad cracked his head on the two foot ceiling as he jumped out of bed and reached the door in two seconds flat with the Quadruple D

MagLite switched on and ready for attack as some little grey thing went flying twenty-seven feet to our end of the trailer.

Once again, Jared had just cracked his head tumbling from the small opening in the tiny loft/storage cabinet, Robert was yelling something about Effie Lynn and I just sat there in complete shock.

We found the rat! Effie Lynn had more hidden talents! Who knew she made one heck of a fantastic flying squirrel! Such a multi-talented little rat she was...and thank God for that tail because she clung onto the knob on the cabinet of the loft as if she were dangling off the Empire State Building.

Deceptively Effie Lynn Mousekewits had found her way back home. Mom is still convinced Effie Lynn camped out waiting for the right moment to crawl out and avenge her by scaring the living pooh out of her in the middle of the night.

The whole incident was so traumatic for everyone involved that Mr. Babcock agreed to let Effie Lynn live with us instead of coming back to the classroom. Needless to say Dad, Jared and Robert went to work on building a far superior cage that made Alcatraz look like prison for the novice and Effie Lynn Mousekewits became our second family pet.

THE K STANDS FOR KRAP

When I was four years old I was at a park playing in the sandbox when a woman's Doberman Pinscher, which was off leash, came running over and bit me in the eye. The settlement was $500 and was put into a trust account until I was sixteen years old.

$500 in 1984 might have bought something nice. But, in 1995, $500 bought me a 1988 Dodge Aries a few months before my sixteenth birthday, just in time for driver training.

I'm not sure what's worse, the scar under my left eye from the dog or the honkin' piece of junk my parents bought me. I would have given my whole left eye for a Jeep, more specifically a CJ7, but Dad was not having any of that nonsense. So I was stuck with the four-door, slate-blue-meets-gun metal-grey, square box of a quote-end-quote "vehicle" that did not have automatic windows or door locks, or even a cassette player, but came equipped with a heater and five pre-programmed radio stations.

I'd been through the "Basic Drivers 101" class in school and had gotten my learner's permit, which meant I was allowed to drive a car so long as someone over the age of twenty-five with a valid drivers license was in the car with me. RIGHT! Completely logical, because it's so much better when there is someone in the car to witness the drama versus innocent bystanders simply catching glimpses of the chaos and madness.

Mom and Dad drew straws on who would teach me how to drive. Mom lost, and so she was my driving instructor. I love Mom, do not get me wrong, however, at fifteen, I believed Mom was completely overrated and yelled at me enough as it was. Being trapped in a car with her for driver training was miserable.

Driver training with Mom began like this, "Michaela, it's really important you don't drive like me. Controlled recklessness will come later, with time. For now, it's important that you learn how to drive safely and defensively, especially on these mountain roads."

And with that, we were headed to the "city" also known as "off the hill" for Starbucks and shopping with the "blue hair's" at Gottshalks, or at least cruising the parking lot of the strip mall. The goal was to get there without the use of an ambulance or a tow truck.

In Georgetown, driver training involves hairpin turns, an occasional half mile straight away with a jerk who has a lead foot passing you screaming "go back to San Francisco Ass Wipe!" plus the added benefit of complete darkness-no streetlights and abundant deer who find vehicular headlights as alluring as mosquitoes to the bug zapper. One tiny wrong maneuver will have you careening off a 700 foot cliff to the bottom of the American River.

For a first time driver, the journey is terrifying. We headed down Highway 193 and into the Auburn Ravine to make the trek to Auburn. Locals know this stretch of the highway as "the Canyon," which is a good descriptor because if you close your eyes and envision things like Thelma and Louise, Donner

Summit, Yellowstone and the Grand Canyon that's probably about right.

It's a winding, twisting two-lane road with a double yellow line separating on-coming traffic (which is really more of a suggestion) and a guard rail or two in a few of the worst spots that wouldn't stop a five-year old on a set of big-wheels.

We made the first tight corner and began to drop into the curvy canyon. I was intently concentrating on being the safest driver on the road when Mom started in on me, "Please downshift."

But she asked me in the middle of the turn, which was more than I could process.

"Please don't tell me what to do; I'm trying to focus here." I replied.

"I will tell you what to do, that's why it's called 'training.' You're going to wear out the brakes."

I rolled my eyes.

She gave me a look that said, "If you weren't driving with the potential of us going off the cliff I'd kick your butt right now," but she remained quiet and calm.

I kept glancing nervously in the rear view mirror and began to realize there were a good sixteen or so cars piled up behind me. Finally I broke the silence.

"This jerk is riding my ass." I stated.

Mom looked at me in complete and total shock. I was quite proud of the affect my comment had on her. All this time she thought I never paid attention to anything her and Dad said. Of course I did! I heard it and I even retained it for later use! Imagine that!

I'd also picked up a few others over the years that I would save for other appropriate driving moments.

"How many cars are there? If there are more than six you need to pull over." Mom replied.

"Um, like twelve…"

"Pull over."

"Yeah right, Mom. There's no good spots to pull over."

"You see the yellow signs? They give you advance notice of good spots. Look, there's a turn out in ¼ mile."

A quarter mile comes pretty darn quick…well in a car anyway. I mean, it takes a good three minutes on foot, I figured I had at least that… So I just blew past it, on accident of course.

"YOU PASSED IT. PULL OVER."

"NO DUH."

It seems that the words "no" and "duh" as a combination are enough to send my mother over the edge. Because of all of a sudden, she was literally screaming at me to pull over and let the cars go by. But there was absolutely no safe location! Literally every turnout was filled with gravel and would put the car far too close to the edge of the cliff. So I did the only logical thing. I sped up.

"MICHAELA, SLOW DOWN AND PULL THIS CAR OVER RIGHT NOW."

"No!" I screamed.

"Right now!"

"MOM! You don't have a brake! Quit hitting the floor like that!"

"Michaela Renee, I'm going to break something as soon as you pull this car over!"

There was squealing, jerking and shaking, and then there was the sounds the car was making too. When we got to the bottom of the canyon I pulled the car over and put it in park. Mom threw open the door and politely walked around the front of the car glaring me down the entire way. She yanked open my door and said, "GET OUT."

I obliged because like my car she is also an Aries, known in the astrology world as a ram, and she was serious. She turned the car around and in her controlled reckless manner brought that four-banger skidding up the driveway.

We jumped out and raced towards the trailer huffing and puffing where Dad and the boys had the TV tray set up like a poker table. Apparently there were some mileage bets on just how far Mom and I would make it.

"You will NOT believe what YOUR daughter just did." Mom accused.

"Um, excuse me, for the record…I have proof from Roseville hospital in the form of a birth certificate with little feet and your signature that you are in fact my mother, and I drive exactly like YOU. I'm sorry if you can't handle it. Now you know how the rest of us feel." I argued back.

That was when Dad became my driving instructor.

Dad dragged me out to the driveway with the boys trailing behind him. I'm not sure if they were actually interested in Dad's lesson or were just tired of hearing Mom's over-the-top rant about her near death experience.

Since Dad had an audience he started with the basics-in other words the car did not leave the driveway for a *really* long time.

He began by walking around the car pointing out all the features like "hood release" and "tire pressure gauge" and their added benefits like "popping the hood" and "making sure the tires were full."

Whatever.

All I really wanted to know was how to set the five pre-programmed positions on the radio dial. My eyes started to glaze over when he got to the whole oil part but I did commit to memory him doing something with the dipstick, because that was pretty official looking. He also made sure to mention that the horn was a critical part of defensive driving, and to not be afraid to use it if other driver's on the road were risking my life. Ok. Noted.

Evidently my lack of interest was not missed by my father, because he suddenly left. The boys kept circling the car like vultures on a carcass. When Dad returned Jared looked over at him and said, "Hey Dad…What's the "K" stand for?"

Dad went into some ridiculously long detail about the "K-model" saving Chrysler from bankruptcy in the late 80's.

"Naturally, yet another brilliant idea to save someone from bankruptcy." I snapped referencing the trailer situation Dad had landed us in to avoid declaring his own bankruptcy.

"Keep talking like that, Miss Priss, and we'll just park this car in the yard until your brothers are old enough to drive and you can take the bus. I'm sure you're brothers would appreciate it."

Let's see, a Wee Chateau, a trailer and a Dodge Aries K car. Fantastic, can't wait to see the Prom pictures.

Jared and Robert looked suddenly very scared and sympathetic and mumbled something about it being a really cool car.

While I was distracted visualizing my Junior Prom date, the K Car and the Wee Chateau, Dad proceeded to open the driver door and do the unthinkable…he took a stick-it note and duct taped it to the dash. The boys and I immediately ventured closer to the passenger window and peered in. It read:

SIS -CHECK OIL WITH EVERY FILL UP,
IF LOW BUY A QT and TOP OFF.

Are you kidding me? As if driving a gawd-awful blue/grey, four door Aries K car that looked like the one the police use in CSI movies for drug busts wasn't enough, now I had a neon stick-it on the dash making it look like I should be riding the short bus instead of driving at all??

"Hop in the driver's seat, Sis!" Dad said.

The boys were snickering in the background as I struggled to regain a shred of dignity and put the keys in the ignition.

Dad's driver training began with a field trip to all the important driver destinations, such as "Chester Fried Chicken, Library and Petrol" and "Murchies Auto Garage, Tow and Hair Care."

Since there is only one highway in town, and there is only one place where two roads cross. The journey to the gas station was simple. I only had to pull into traffic on one occasion, then it was a straight shot up the Highway towards Main Street/downtown Georgetown- three minutes and it'd be all over.

As I approached the stop sign I glanced over toward Dad and asked the burning question, "How it's URINE WAY Pee Pee?"

"Yellow, you gotta red CJ5 coming fast, and a white Honda Accord, after that you're runnin' clear."

As long as I was in the driver's seat, Dad was treating me like a real grown up. We were in business. Within one and a half minutes we were pulling into the gas station.

I didn't get Starbucks, but I did get a pretty amazing sixteen-ounce house blend in a beautiful styrofoam cup. Dad even suggested the French vanilla creamer, which made me feel like an adult.

A few months of driver training passed. During that time the K car started making a pretty hefty knocking sound. I figured since no one mentioned it, I wouldn't either. I had started to become fond of my little car and its unlimited freedom potential.

My sixteenth birthday was scheduled to fall on Thanksgiving which presented a small problem.

Since the Department of Motor Vehicles was going to be closed in observance of the holiday, I placed a few calls to the federal government to see if we could get the date moved and accommodate an appointment for my driver's license test but I had zero luck, apparently the Pilgrims were pretty set on that whole "fourth thursday of November" thing for the founding of America and so are the lazy federal employees.

So I settled for the first appointment they had following the holiday. I must say, the whole test went pretty well until I drove over the curb.

Fortunately for me, I corrected the steering wheel which meant I didn't get an automatic fail, and if it weren't for that one little hiccup I would have had a perfect score... it appears that the DMV considers driving over the curb a pretty big deal though so I lost twelve points, which meant I still passed, but barely.

Really who cares if it's one point or twelve? A "pass" whether it's "barely" or "not" means, "WATCH OUT pedestrians – I'm LEGAL!"

It was my first official day driving to school on my own- no Dad rambling technical details about the four cylinder engine versus a six cylinder, no insane Mother slamming her foot into a non existent floor pedal...just me, New Country 105.1 and Shania Twain singing "Any Man of Mine" at the top of our lungs.

School let out and I was pretty excited to walk to the parking lot instead of to the bus line. Everyone knew I'd just passed the big D-Test and I'd been getting congratulations in the hall all day. I turned the ignition threw the car in reverse and started to drive out of the lot with the other kids who had cars. Parked in the line waiting to exit the high school I heard someone honk. I wasn't really sure who honked, but I smiled and waved anyway.

As I started to make the right turn onto the highway, I heard someone else honk. Everyone was so sweet. It certainly was a big deal to have your license and be driving, after all. This time I cranked the window down, smiled and waved my hand furiously.

Goodbye! First day leaving School as a new driver! This was awesome! I was elated!

As I pulled onto the open highway I jacked up the stereo pretty loud, this time I was tuned into Alice 97.3 and Gavin Rossdale of Bush was helping my nine-mile journey home. The song ended and the funniest thing happened, I heard someone honk again.

I glanced in the rear view and out each of my side windows to confirm, that in fact, there were no cars on the road around me. How odd, I thought.

I hit my own horn and realized the tonality was quite similar, but I just went ahead and turned up the radio, which I had seen Mom do a few times when the knocking of the engine got too loud.

As I approached the stop sign in the middle of Main Street Georgetown it struck me. It was completely unmistakable. My horn was honking itself. I was behind two cars in line at the four-way intersection and Chester Fried Chicken and Petrol was full of kids from my school filling up their cars. Everyone looked over as my car continually honked its own horn.

So I did the only thing anyone would have done, I turned up the radio even louder and flipped them all off. By the time I was pulling up the driveway I was pissed. The horn would not stop. The boys came running out of the trailer.

"What do you want, Kayla?" Jared screamed.

"Yeah, Sissy, stop honking!" Robert finished.

"Screw you guys!" I hollered back. "LOOKIE! NO FREAKING HANDS!"

The boys' jaws dropped in awe. I threw the car in park and turned off the ignition and the car gave one more honk just for good measure. By this point the boys were on the ground in the middle of the driveway laughing hysterically.

"Oh sure. See if I EVER give either of you a ride." I said.

"Do us a favor," Jared said. "Don't EVER pick us up from school."

Dad and Mom got home from work about the same time that night, apparently someone had already called Mom from Chester Fried Chicken to tell her I was driving recklessly and honking the horn uncontrollably.

Jared and Robert were dying to tell them the whole story, starting with how I thought I was 'so cool' at school and that everyone was honking at me but I was honking at myself. I pretty much became ridiculously annoyed when the snorting ensued and ended the entire conversation by screaming at the top of my lungs, "HEY DAD, THE HORN DUN WORKS REAL GOOD – OH AND PS – CHRYSLER CALLED- THE K STANDS FOR KRAP!"

And then I stormed to the driveway, turned on the car, jacked up the heater and sat there with the windows hand cranked up and the doors locked for a good thirty minutes with the radio blaring on one of the five preset radio stations attempting to drown out the incessant honking.

GEORGETOWN STREET LUGE

The foundation to the house had been sitting for quite some time; by some time, I mean over two years. Dad had finally saved up enough money to purchase the supplies necessary to frame the house. I think he'd been keeping the dough in a tin can buried underneath the fifth wheel of the trailer, he certainly wasn't trusting any banks with his money after the economic collapse. Literally eight-thousand dollars, our entire life savings, just enough to buy the wood.

Dad and I were out in the driveway, I had popped the hood to the K for Krap car and he was ripping the wire to the horn connection so I could get to and from school and work without the incessant honking. As I watched him tinker around under the hood I said, "Heaven forbid I need that horn for defensive driving because I'll have to scream and curse at the top of my lungs and flip the birdie instead."

"No you won't, you'll just drive safely and you won't need the horn."

"Sure, ok Dad. Whatever."

"Listen," Dad began, "I've got a really important delivery coming today. Georgetown Divide Supply is dropping off the wood so we can start framing the house this weekend. Please park your car down the driveway away so they can drop it off as close to the foundation as possible."

"Sure, no problem." I told him and then I headed to work hornless.

I had been working nights and weekends at the Papa's Pizzeria for the last few months (babysitting just wasn't covering enough of the expenses around the house and my new K for Krap car costs) and had just started a second job working as a typesetter for the Georgetown Gazette. Mark Lance (the owner) had heard about my interest in writing from my Mom and offered me the minimum wage job as experience more than anything. I was giddy at any opportunity to learn more about the newspaper business and certainly didn't mind the extra cash either, so I put in two hours a day right after school, and then went to the Papa's Pizzeria to work my night shift.

As I pulled the K for Krap car into Chester Fried Chicken and Petrol and filled up; the yellow stick it note reminded me to check the oil. I slowly lifted the dipstick and sure enough, it was a quart low, again. It was the third time this week! I went in and purchased my usual, a quart of oil, Mountain Dew and butterscotch candy. This whole car expense thing was getting outrageous.

By the time I got done dealing with the oil I was five minutes late for my job at the Gazette, when I rolled in I had butterscotch clanking around in my mouth. My boss laughed at me when I told him my K for Krap car was acting up. He seemed to enjoy my endless nutty stories and there wasn't anything in the office he didn't teach me how to do. I followed him around, soaking it all up like a sponge. We received about fifty faxes a day at the Gazette, everything from advertisements, to Associated Press stories to fictitious business names, birth and death announcements. We also received a lot of community awareness articles. It was my job to sort through all the faxes and determine which would get published and which would not, and then I would literally retype every fax into the old 1986 Macintosh so that it could be dropped into the PageMaker program we used to layout the newspaper.

I guzzled some Mountain Dew to wash down the butterscotch and made my way over to the fax machine. With my purse still over my shoulder I began to flip through the faxes. I nearly spit Mountain Dew everywhere when I saw it:

MISS ELDORADO COUNTY PAGEANT COMPETITION SEEKS...

It was followed by audition information and the requirements, which included drumming up $2,000 in sponsorships. The winner of the pageant landed a scholarship to college as well as other exciting things and of course the prestigious title and tiara. I immediately walked the paperwork over to Meg and Wendy (who completed our entire staff of four), and extended my reach as far as possible to dangle the fax in front of them.

El Dorado County is by no means Los Angeles County but being from Georgetown, one of the smaller towns, definitely put me at a disadvantage.

"Do it!" They both exclaimed at the same time.

College was creeping up quickly and come hell or high water I was going. With Mom and Dad barely having enough money to frame the house, there was absolutely zero expectation of them being able to help me. If I won the competition, it'd be my ticket out of town.

So I'm on my way home from work, elated about trying out for the competition when I see this blur go speeding by me the opposite direction. It was zipping by at about 27mph, screaming down the main road to town and it was loaded up like the Grinch's Christmas sleigh toppling with kids. In the pilot and co-pilot seats were my two brothers.

"What was THAT?" I thought as I flipped around in my seat straining my neck to verify that in fact my brothers were driving it.

As I pulled up in the driveway I noticed that there had been a neatly stacked bundle of two by four studs, beams and other items, but now, it had been picked apart the way a bear goes through trash in a camp ground and was scattered everywhere.

In this moment I realized what had happened. And this time Robert was not just an accomplice to Jared's creation, they both spearheaded the project together.

They had busted into Dad's neatly stacked $8,000 life savings and decided to build some mode of transportation to show up my K for Krap car.

One of us was going to be seriously reamed when Dad got home. About that time I hear a bunch of kids coming up the driveway laughing louder than a GTO without an exhaust pipe.

It was the most impressive piece of architectural design I have ever seen. As I watched them wheel the thing up the driveway I choked back my laughter and put on my meanest face and began to demand an explanation.

"Jared! Did you use Dad's wood to build that thing?"

"That THING is a GO Kart KAYLA!" Jared screamed back.

"I see that…Dad is going to be so ticked off when he gets home."

"There's plenty of wood, Sissy!" Robert chimed in.

Sure, plenty of wood to start a mass production Go Kart facility but NOT plenty of wood to frame a house.

"Where did you guys even get the idea for this?" Now I was pumping questions out of sheer morbid curiosity.

I should have been getting angrier as they told the story, but instead I started laughing realizing Dad would probably get a kick out of this.

As it would turn out when my brothers were in San Luis Obispo a few weeks before they had gotten to ride my cousin's real Go Karts. Between that and the sprint cars they'd seen racing they had a good idea of the design. They spent the entire five hour drive home on Interstate 5 brainstorming the design for the masterpiece. When the wood got delivered Jared saw it as a sign from the Heavens and called up half the neighborhood to get it built. We might have been poor, but we were not lacking in creativity.

They took a four by four post, ten feet long, drilled a hole in the front, put a locknut with washers and a two by four post horizontally in front and the rear so they could steer. Then they'd taken five plastic lawn chairs and bolted them to the four by four post chassis, one right after the other, follow the leader style. There was a rope that the pilot used to steer the two by four in the front and the seat in the back had two- two by four's straight down to the ground, with old rubber tires screwed to the bottom creating a lever action E Brake. Supporting the entire structure and creating mobility was four sets of skateboarding truck wheels for a total of eight wheels, which were mounted to each corner of the front and back two by four's. Robert had assigned one of his friends to paint it, the kid did the best he could with the limited supplies. He stole Dad's spray paint cans and painted the whole Kart beautiful orange and green two-tone.

And there stood a Go Kart good enough to hold it's own at a NASCAR event, completely hand made out of yard scraps by my two little brothers and their friends in less than a day.

They were using the main drag to MarVal as a real life street luge. The Kart held a total of five kids but only two were required to drive it. The first journey down to MarVal was an absolute success, the design was flawless. So much so, that even adults coming out of the store with grocery bags were requesting rides.

Robert (who was already developing an entrepreneurial spirit) saw an opportunity to charge for this service and between the two of them they began making a hefty penny on Go Kart rides from the trailer to MarVal.

At this rate, by the time my parents got home they'd have made enough money to replace the plastic lawn chairs that they had stolen, which was really good because that was NOT going to go over well with Mom.

My stomach hurt from laughing so hard, if I couldn't drum up $2,000 in sponsor money for the Pageant maybe Ghetto Go Karts Inc. could float the rest from street loge rides to be a primary sponsor.

I went inside the trailer to start placing sponsorship calls when I heard Dad pull up the driveway. Before he'd even shut the truck off I heard the yelling ensue, "BOYS, WHAT HAVE YOU DONE WITH MY WOOD?"

And the subsequent "but…but Dad…but" justification. They were unsuccessful; I knew it was only a matter of time before I got drug into it.

Sure enough, within minutes Dad was punishing all three of us. We were grounded for a week, and we would all be helping to frame the house the following weekend.

Then Dad saw the Kart and that changed everything. After a complete review from the boys, Dad became impressed with their tenacity, determination and attitude, and in exchange for a Go Kart ride the punishment was lessened to us simply having to help frame the house for the entire weekend.

I, of course, threw a complete hissy fit about the great risks of injury involved with the framing process and the importance of maintaining my youthful beauty and soft hands for the pageant, but that was pretty much completely ignored.

I had a very productive week and by the time Thursday night rolled around I had dumped $25 in oil in the K for Krap car and landed $500 from four sponsors - MarVal Food Stores, Mark A. Smith Real Estate (owner of Jeep Jamboree/ Rubicon Specialists), Beam Dozer and Backhoe Service and Worton's Gold Mine Gift Shop. I submitted my application and completed my first interview for Miss El Dorado County.

I didn't get out of the Papa's Pizzeria until late because a softball team had just won and was drinking pitcher after pitcher of beer. By the time I got to my car I was exhausted and less than thrilled about the funny smell coming from the hood but I just ignored it and headed home. About a ½ mile from the house I started noticing the smoke billowing from the hood, I wasn't stopping now I was almost home. By the time I got to the driveway the K for Krap was barely able to putt, rolling about five miles an hour in first gear, I was screaming "C'MON BESSY!!"

Dad came running out.

"SHUT OFF THE MOTOR!" he yelled.

No duh! I was getting to that. The minute she crept into my spot in the driveway I shut it off and jumped out. I was damn proud. "WHO HOO, SHE MADE IT!" I screamed and skipped around her patting her on the trunk. "Adda Girl!"

Dad was unimpressed. "MICHAELA - Have you been putting oil in this thing like I showed you?"

"YES, DAD!"

"How much?"

"I've been putting a full QUART A DAY!!" I screamed at him.

"WHAT?" Dad yelled back.

"Oh my God! Michaela! Your BLONDE is showing!" Mom joined in.

Okay, for the record, no where on the stick it note did it say, "if you begin to need to add more than a quart every day then there is a problem." I mean, perhaps he should be a little more clear with his instructions.

I told him that, but he wasn't very pleased with that piece of information.

Dad spent a few hours under the hood of my car, while I sat in a plastic lawn chair shining a Maglite watching my brothers cruise up and down the street in the GO Kart in the dark, which was a heck of a lot further than my car was moving. I figured this whole thing was a Darwin award waiting to happen when Dad finally slammed the hood shut and turned around.

"You got any plans tomorrow night?" Dad asked.

"Yeah."

"Work?"

"No."

"Alright then, cancel it. We're going to the Pick-N-Pull, we need parts for this thing."

What in God's name was the Pick-N-Pull and why did I have to go? I mean, if the boys could build a Go Kart out of material lying around the house, why did I have to go to the Pick-N-Pull to fix my car? Apparently the Pick-N-Pull was in order because the K for Krap's engine had blown up. Great.

So here is it, Friday night, Dad and I- an Almost-Miss-El-Dorado-Pageant Princess- en route to the junkyard. A few hours later under the blaring football stadium-esq florescent lights of Jerry's Used Automotive and U-Pick-It we were pulling apart an engine from a burgundy Plymouth Reliant. I don't know much about Plymouth, except that the Pilgrims landed at a rock with the same name some 200 years before, this car *looked* about that old. In other words, it made my K for Krap car look borderline amazing.

Dad was rambling on about how this engine was almost identical to the one in the K for Krap car and that we would get an A-frame and swap the engines. All I was hearing was NO transportation to and from work and school and my pageant and all I could wonder was how much my brothers were going to charge me for rides on the GO Kart. Life was beginning to look pretty gloomy.

The next morning I woke up to George Strait hollerin somethin' about calling him the Firemun and a crew full of people in the front yard. Dad had done a fair amount of favors in his day and there was no shortage of people who were willing to spend a weekend helping us frame the house. If for nothing other than pity people wanted to see us upgrade from Trailer Trash status.

The worst part of framing was mounting the Glue-Lam beam. It was thirty feet long, six inches wide and eighteen inches tall. It's literally ten two by six boards laminated together and it weighs over five-hundred pounds.

Its job is to support the ceiling joists and provide bracing for the roof structure. Which meant we had to hoist it up, some nine feet in the air and hold it in place while the crew secured it down. It literally took more than six of us, over two hours of excruciating, back pain causing, sweat dripping, manual labor to get it locked and loaded.

But by the end of the weekend we'd completed the majority of framing and there stood the skeleton of a real life house. I was bruised up, and had no fingernails left, but it didn't matter. Dad and Mom had been saving for such a long time, what quite frankly felt like forever, and to see the beginning of our house was exhilarating. To know that we had done it together was even more impressive. All of our sweat and tears had gone into the basic framework that would become our future home.

It was nothing more than a foundation and a bunch of two by four's, but it was hope. Hope that we would not be living in the trailer forever. Hope that we would someday live like 'normal people' again.

In the three weeks following the framing of the house I bummed rides from friends, and hoofed it to and from work. Every day when Dad got off work, he'd recruit me and the boys to help put in a few hours on the house, and then we'd put in a few hours on the engine to my car. Progress was slow.

By the time the Pageant rolled around school had just let out for summer and I'd cleaned up pretty well. The mud was gone from under my finger nails, I had been properly degreased of car gunk and the rough patches of skin on my palms from the two by four's had been sloughed off. I had heard some girls talking at one of the rehearsals a few days before, about the politics and the fact that one of the girl's Daddy's was running for City Council and would probably win because of it, but I didn't have much time to get caught up in that and just went about my business.

I'd done the best job I could to prepare given the fact that I was working two jobs, carrying A's in my classes and helping Dad fix my engine and build a house in what little spare time I had.

The whole family had turned out to support me and right before I went backstage Dad's Mom (my grandma) had said, whatever you do, no matter how nervous you get, don't hunch – stand up tall! At 5'9, I was accustomed to crouching down to match the height of most of the people around me, but today I felt like a million dollars and it showed when I stepped on stage to deliver my speech.

My nervousness was replaced with pride when I got to the masking tape line on the black platform and saw my grandma in the crowd, she was beaming. I rolled my shoulders back and stood tall and proud. I knew for a fact I was the only girl who could back up every word I spoke, and I was definitely the only girl who had hung nine feet in the air holding a Glue Lam beam and crawled underneath the hood of a car at the Pick-N-Pull in the four weeks before the pageant. I delivered the speech with perfection and a huge smile.

The pageant drug on for what felt like hours. Finally the last routine came around, it was a group dance that all the girls did in matching costumes. Our costumes were 40's saloon skirts that twirled beautifully and were made out of a shiny colorful material by one of the other girl's mom's. Each of us were specially fitted and sized for our final dance routine.

We went out on the stage and Travis Tritt's "Trouble" stared blaring from the sound equipment, 5-6-7-8. Having cheerleading experience meant I was good at retaining and executing a dance routine, before I knew it I was really into the song and kickin' up my knickers. Just seconds before the end of the routine all of us girls came together to a fouette kick line.

I threw my arm around the girl next to me and started, knee up, kick up, knee up, kick up. Then all of a sudden I felt a lot of cold air in places it shouldn't be. That's when I realized what had happened. I had kicked my skirt off. The whoops and hollers began and I realized that the Velcro (which they selected for quick dress change in between the formal gown delivery speech and dance routine) was not strong enough for my cheerleading professional super high fouette kick!

With the reflexes of a cat I clutched for my skirt and with zero grace managed to get some part of it dangling around my butt while the rest of the skirt flapped in the wind, like something Vera Wang would have designed for the cat walk. I finished the dance number with a death grip around a miniscule shred of material, at the end I took a curtsy and blew a kiss. I glanced up just in time to see the mortified expressions of both Mom's parents and Dad's Mom. Great.

As we stood in a row waiting for the names to be called I heard them begin the runners up announcement. I'll admit after my little on stage escapades I was quite surprised to hear them call my name at all, let alone award me "Best in Poise and Best in Personality." But as I walked to the podium to accept my award deep down I knew while that was wonderful, it wasn't enough to send me to college. Sure enough the girl whose Daddy was running for City Council was crowned the 1996 Miss El Dorado Pageant Princess.

I hugged and kissed the other girls without shedding a tear and then quickly left. I wanted it and needed it more than all of them, not for the tiara (that was a nice addition) but for the scholarship. The moment I closed the door to my parents Jeep I began to cry, and through my blurry tear stained eyes I turned around in the back seat to see the "Moving Day Posse" behind us. Mom had had faith in me and planned some really nice "after pageant" party, as if I would have had the tiara on, and all of our friends and family were following us home from the Fair to show support for my failed attempt at a college education. All I wanted to do was crawl under a rock and hide. As if getting "Best in Poise" and "Best in Personality" wasn't bad enough, now my entire family and extended family and friends had seen my under panties.

I put on a smiley face and tried to be chipper and thankful for the fact that everyone was there for me, and that meant a lot. Mom had set up the party in the area of the framed house that would be our future kitchen. She really did a beautiful job of making it look fit for a princess. As much as my pride stung from the pageant loss, I was really happy we weren't sitting around in plastic lawn chairs in the dirt. At least we had a cement foundation and some semblance of walls at our party.

My grandparents had come over to congratulate me… Papa had gotten me one dozen roses. They were proud regardless of the loss, I'm pretty sure though there's something in the grandparent user manual that says, they have to be happy for you no matter what. Nanny and Papa saw my K for Krap car with the A-frame squatting over the top of the hood and an engine dangling down and asked me how'd I'd been getting to school and work. I told them, bummin' rides and walking. I wasn't sure where they were going with that, but I wasn't sure I wanted to know either. So I just politely excused myself and went back to the buffet table Mom had set up.

I had consumed three slices of pizza and was gulping grape soda straight out of the bottle feeling pretty depressed when Robert tapped me on the shoulder.

I turned around. He had a little shiny piece of metal in his hand.

"Bend down, Sissy," he said.

So I did, and as I tilted my head forward, he slipped on a tiara that he and Jared had made for me from the framing scraps. As I stood back up I started to cry again and he gave me a big hug. "See, now you are a princess," he whispered. As I turned around I saw that Jared had brought the Go Kart around.

"Hop in, Kayla, we're taking you for a ride on the back!" Jared exclaimed.

"Like the princesses do in the parade!" Robert yelled.

It was kind of silly, but they were so excited and I actually had been so busy that I hadn't ridden in the GO Kart yet. So I started down the driveway and Robert hopped in the front. I climbed in the back, with my makeshift tiara on.

Mom and Dad came around the corner just in time to witness it and Mom yelled, "Don't forget to do the pageant wave!"

And then Jared yelled, "Oh yea, and you have to operate the E-brake since you're riding in the back."

With one hand waving to the "Moving Day Posse" and the other on the two by four-rubber tire E-brake I realized I could figure out a back up plan for college tomorrow, today I was the princess. The boys jerked the thing in motion and I nearly toppled out as we headed down the street for MarVal, I'd roll in and thank them for the sponsorship while I was there.

SANTA AND THE HOT BATH

I walked out to the driveway and attempted to unlock my driver's side door, the key wouldn't budge in the K for Krap car. Ever since we'd gotten the Plymouth Reliant's engine dropped in nothing was working. Who cares that the door lock has nothing to do with the engine; the reality is the car was rejecting its new engine and taking it out on me in whatever way possible.

It was snowing outside; Dad had gone down to the Ace Hardware in town a couple of week's earlier and purchased three space heaters to keep us warm inside the trailer. Just moments before as I lifted one of them up off the ground I felt that it was light which meant that the five gallon propane tank for the water heater to the trailer was also nearly empty, if not bone dry. I'm not sure there was much worse than that. On top of it I couldn't even unlock my car to get the propane tanks down to Ace Hardware to be refilled.

At the time I didn't think to go around to the passenger side door and attempt to unlock it, instead I just gave up and went back inside the trailer. Mom and Dad should be home soon anyways.

I was pretty miserable knowing that I needed to shower, it was snowing outside, the space heater and water heater were almost out of propane.

I looked over at the boys who were playing Rummy with a deck of cards on the table tray to the light of a kerosene lantern.

"Boys, there's not much propane in here."

"Go ahead Kayla, I'm not going to shower tonight." Jared said as he slapped a spread down on the makeshift table.

"Me either, Sissy," Robert added as he hit on Jared's spread.

I looked over at their dirty feet and hands; I could barely make out two pairs of glistening blue eyes through the dirt creating a raccoon mask around their pudgy cheeks. I lifted the space heater and took it into the bathroom.

The space was so tiny that the only place I could set it was on the toilet. And while the snow outside was magical; the temperature of the water inside was the exact same temperature as the snow which made it a lot less alluring. I turned on the shower head to rinse down and let out a shrill equivalent to one Jamie Lee Curtis let out in the horror flicks.

I'd learned from experience that shaving your legs in snowmelt water was a bloody mess, so I passed on that and on washing my hair too. If your head is that cold, it takes hours to warm up, and there wasn't enough propane to take us through the night.

The house was coming along really nicely, and the shower-tub combo had already been installed with part of the framing of the house. Dad had even built a small shed outside the trailer that would act as a place to hold additional clothing, and eventually a full size refrigerator, a washer and a dryer. As I snuggled into the sleeping bag that night I pictured the tub sitting out there in the snow and realized that sooner than later that would be a real bathroom, with hot running water.

A week later was like Christmas in November at the trailer. The permits had come through for water and electric. The five of us spent every spare minute trenching a line from the street to the trailer and the frame of the house. The process was incredibly time consuming and it did not appear as thought progress was being made. We'd finally laid all the conduit lines and I'll never forget the day we saw the bright blue PG&E truck pull up the driveway. We sat silent as the supervisor trolled through the trenches with his clipboard. It's hard not to act desperate when you've lived without running water or electricity for that long.

Finally, after an incredibly long silence he looked up from his clipboard and said, "Looks good." And then he signed off on it.

We were ecstatic. Over the weekend Dad pulled the wires through the conduits. Sunday morning was like that scene from Chevy Chase when they all go outside to watch Clark Griswold light up the house in eager excitement for feeling holiday cheer while we waited for Dad to finishing hooking up the temporary meter box.

The moment prior was eerily silent; primarily there was no hum of a generator in the background. We all waited patiently. This was it, no more propane space heaters, no more ice chests to cool our perishable foods, no more kerosene lanterns for light at night.

Dad flicked the breaker and it was if the trailer came to life. Suddenly the tiny refrigerator was making sputting noises, the light bulbs flickered and the heater made popping sounds. Mom walked over to the sink and twisted the knob and she didn't shut it off either. We had running water, a gorgeous unlimited supply of flowing liquid.

Later that afternoon I was sitting in the Wee Chateau, as we still didn't have a septic system waiting for my pee to trickle, which was a process in and of itself because the toilet seat was as cold as sitting on an ice cube, when I overheard Mom and Dad's conversation.

Mom was elated about the water and the power but she told Dad the one thing she really missed the most was taking a bath. It was hard seeing the framing of the house and the tub sitting there all by its lonesome, but with a five gallon propane tank and no septic system she wouldn't be getting a bath any time soon. As I peeled my butt from the plastic seat of the porta-potty I realized the one thing I really missed was being able to unlock the driver's side door of my car like a normal person, instead I had to do a ridiculous run around to the passenger side, reach over the mile long bench seat unlock job from the inside then scoot over to the passenger side or run back around to the drivers side routine every time I wanted to drive somewhere. My request was a lot easier to attain but since Dad had a bazillion other things going on I didn't dare ask him to help me fix it.

The Christmas holiday was quickly approaching and now that we had electricity we had the ability to watch shows on the tiny TV. The boys and I were watching "A Christmas Story" and "Charlie Brown Christmas" specials when they began the big debate over whether or not there was a Santa Claus.

They were getting to the age where kids at school were starting rumors that Santa didn't really exist.

"Sissy…do you think there's a Santa?" Robert asked.

"Of course." I told Robert, "If there wasn't a Santa how do you think we got any gifts at all? Mom and Dad don't have money for gifts."

"Nuh uh Kayla, Dad IS Santa," Jared demanded.

Robert was stuck in the middle and very confused, so I continued.

"Look, if Dad was Santa, don't you think you'd have heard him? It's not like the trailer is very big," I finished.

Robert was searching mine and Jared's faces for an answer, but he wouldn't be getting one from me anyway.

The night before Christmas Eve we'd gotten a hellacious storm which had dumped a lot of snow. I got a phone call that some of the people from school who were gathering up a crew to go Snow-Wheelin. I was always up for a good time and I didn't have to work at the Papa's Pizzeria until the evening, I was closing since it was a holiday and I was youngest on the totem pole.

Snow-Wheelin is similar to 4-Wheelin, except it's done in the snow. The entire goal is to take the 4-wheel-drive trucks past the snow plow line and get stuck, and then we rinse and repeat. Once we've gotten as far as we possibly can, we turn the trucks around and hook up the sleds with rope to the tow hitch and ride back home.

When I got home that afternoon I had literally an hour before I had to be at work. The boys had created their own fun in the snow, and they were excited to show me. After much arm pulling they convinced me to head down to the irrigation ditch where they'd carved a massive slope out of the hill. In the summer time we used the irrigation ditch for tubing. We had some old rubber intertubes with holes that we'd duct taped. We'd launch the tube down the ditch rolling five deep it was so weighted down in some spots the bottom of the tube was scraping the bottom of the ditch which inevitably would land us hole or two. We became professional tube pluggers, we got so good that we could plug them with our fingers and finish the ride.

By the time we got down there the ditch looked more like a river, complete with white caps and all. The boys started daring each other to jump across the ditch. I had little faith they would make it and knew that missing the landing would make for a very crappy afternoon. But after watching the boys do it, and knowing my legs were twice as long I agreed to the challenge.

I decided a running start would be the best strategy for clearing the ditch. I backed up a good five feet and became very nervous. As I started my sprint nerves took over. The boys were screaming "JUMP, KAYLA!"

But I spotted a bush right at the edge of the ditch and at the last second I decided to back out of the dare, I put the brakes on and attempted to use the bush to slow me down.

With the bush between my legs and both hands gripping it at the base it started to tear out of the ground. Next thing I know I'm face first in the bottom of the irrigation ditch with my extra long (made for jumping) legs sticking straight in the air.

As I drug myself out of the ditch I still had the little bush in my hands. My brothers looked like they were laying in the snow making angels, but in reality they were flopping around on the ground laughing at me.

I trudged home with little under a half hour before I had to be at work, mud was still in my hair from the bottom of the ditch. As I got in the shower in the trailer I realized I had learned something very important. With a continual stream of water coming out of the shower head I could finally get the mud out of my hair and actually get clean and secondly, I had absolutely nothing to complain about, because in fact the water in the shower was a lot warmer than snowmelt.

The storm had passed and the sky was clear as glass, which meant it was also freezing. As I started to close out the register at Papa's Pizzeria I realized I had better go get the car warmed up, the new engine took forever to get fired up, especially in the bitter cold.

I ran out and unlocked the passenger side door, reached over to the ignition, put the key in and turned it; it took a few seconds for the engine to turn over. With my butt end freezing because it was still hanging out of the passenger door I quickly jumped back, relocked and slammed the door shut, then I ran back inside the Papa's Pizzeria. In a small town we never had to worry about things like leaving a car running in a parking lot and no one would want my K for Krap car anyway.

I closed up the Papa's Pizzeria and rushed out to my car, sprinting, but carefully treading so not to slip on the black ice. I walked to the door and attempted to open it and realized that in my rushing haste earlier, I had forgotten to unlock the driver's side door. No problem I thought as I headed around to the passenger side. I felt my heart drop as I lifted the handle to the passenger side door and realized what I'd done.

I stepped back and took a moment to survey the situation. Yes, I had in fact locked my keys in the K for Krap car with the engine running with a full tank of gas in the middle of Papa's Pizzeria parking lot on Christmas Eve.

I went back inside and attempted to call Mom and Dad, the phone rang off the hook. I sat inside for a good thirty minutes trying the phone calls over and over and over. With a full tank of gas that car wasn't going to be puttering out any time soon and so I finally went over to the soda machine and filled it half way with Sprite, then I went over to the wine tap and topped off my cup. As long as I was going to be sitting alone inside Papa's Pizzeria on Christmas Eve I might as well be drinking, who cares that I wasn't twenty-one yet, it was a holiday after all. Another twenty minutes went by and I continually dialed with no answer from the other end.

Where were the boys, and where were my parents? I started to become concerned that they had already left to my Grandma's house in the city for Christmas Eve festivities and that I would be spending the evening alone at Papa's Pizzeria drinking home grown wine coolers. I began to debate leaving the car with the engine running and walking home when Dad finally answered the phone.

"Thank God!" I started.

"Shouldn't you be home by now?" Dad said.

"You won't believe what I did…" I trailed off.

"Something tells me your right," Dad finished.

He cut me off half way through my explanation with, "Only you, Sis," which I didn't have to be in person to know was accompanied by a head scratch and shake, "I'll be there in a few minutes."

Dad and I stood out in the cold as he used a Slim Jim to attempt to pop the lock to the K for Krap car. We pretty much looked like a bunch of thugs attempting to steal the lamest car of all time ever. As I stood there shivering I got peeved at the entire situation and finally asked Dad why no one had answered the phone for the last hour.

Naturally, he had a very good excuse. Turns out Dad had managed to ship the boys off to my Grandma's house right after I'd left for work and then he'd made a pit stop off at the Home Depot.

He purchased a thirty-five gallon hot water heater, which he'd set up outside the trailer while Mom was working her second job in the city. He then ran two garden hoses from the hot water heater near the trailer to the tub in the framed house and filled the bathtub with piping hot water.

He hung a bunch of U-Haul blankets up around the framed walls to close in the bathroom area and lit a bunch of nice smelling candles. He also brought in one of the space heaters and hung a towel nearby so it would be warm.

When she got home that evening, the house was empty, except for Dad who was waiting for her and she'd gotten the best gift of all, a hot bath. Funny thing too, in the process of breaking into the car, he managed to fix my broken lock at the same time, and even though I hadn't believed in Santa for years, tonight I did.

OLD YELLER

The K for Krap car died. That was the end of it. It was parked down the driveway off in the dirt to sit for awhile and I was back to hoofing it and bumming rides to and from work and school.

I probably should have gone straight home after the football game that Friday, but since I didn't have my own car and was riding home with a friend, I didn't have much choice when she suggested that we go down to Canyon Creek (a little high school hideout) to celebrate the recent win. The only way to get there was with a 4-wheel drive, unless you planned on trashing your car.

When we pulled up there was a bunch of people already partying. I spotted him right away. He was tall, about 6'1 had curly blonde hair, the lightest blue eyes I'd ever seen and a smile to stop the presses. Our eyes met and that was pretty much the end of it.

When he started walking towards me, can of Natural Ice in hand, I had already learned that he was nineteen years old, had graduated the year before and had come home because he'd dropped out of college; the rumor was he was sweet, but trouble. I didn't care. I can't even begin to explain what happened in my stomach when he came over and started talking to me. He was into Tom Petty and country music, he drove a 4-wheel drive, he liked to fish and he was smokin' hot.

We kissed that night, and that probably did me in, because he kissed way better than "PottyMouth" (who I'd broken up with a few months before) ever did.

The whole weekend all I could think about was "Trouble" and when I'd get to see him next. My Nanny and Papa had heard about the latest car dilemma, they were always so concerned about my safety and didn't want me to have to worry about silly things like a broken down car. Dad had talked with Papa and worked out a deal to purchase his old 1972 Ford F150. According to the grapevine, the Ford F150, though well over twenty-five years old had been kept in pristine condition and was a reliable mode of transportation.

That was all fine and dandy, but the minute I saw that truck pull up the driveway I really started to miss and appreciate K for Krap. It had been years since I'd ridden in it as a little girl and I'd forgotten how massive it was, not even to mention, it was the brightest color of yellow I have ever seen.

I should have known the destiny of the truck from day one, given that when Dad arrived he had the back loaded with all the parts necessary to install the septic system.

"Dad! That thing is so ugly!" I yelled when he came up the driveway.

"Don't be unappreciative, would you rather walk?" he responded.

"No."

"Alright then, help me unload all these leach fields."

"What is a leach field?" I asked picturing those nasty creatures they used to suck blood from black eyes back in the day.

"It's a critical part of the septic system we're installing. There's the septic tank, the distribution box, and leach fields.

The septic tank holds all the products we flush or rinse through the pipes, the sludge sinks to the bottom and the rest floats to the top. Bacteria mixed with the raw material creates gasses which then vent via the plumbing system. From the septic tank everything that is floating on the top, which is a relatively clear liquid flows into a small distribution box where it is then metered out to perforated pipes. Those pipes are called leach fields, they are for absorption," Dad detailed.

"What happens when it fills up?" I asked.

"Well, that takes years, but same thing as the port-a-potty. We hire a guy with a big truck to come drain it all out," Dad replied.

"Sounds like a crappy job," I laughed.

"Wow, creative. Never heard that joke before," Dad laughed back.

A few weeks later a massive hole was dug in the front yard to hold the septic tank, and a few days after that a massive cement box was dropped in. I guess I was expecting something more sophisticated after all the fancy detailed explanation. The whole thing operated like a big elaborate port-a-potty.

The day Smelly Mel came was a day of rejoicing.

It was a ceremonial ribbon cutting event when Dad finally box cut the duct tape off the toilet in the trailer. A few hours later Smelly Mel arrived to carry away his Wee Chateau to some new location. That port-a-potty had been through a lot with us. From the first time Mom threw the Better Homes and Garden's magazine in the urinal, to the many times I stood outside with a flashlight waiting for Robert who was petrified to take the walk from it to the trailer in the dark on his own, to the numerous fly traps we hung inside, to the time I overheard Mom sharing her wish to have a hot bath (even before a flushing toilet) to Dad.

Life was becoming normal, the house was beginning to look like a real house, and life in the trailer was looking up, we had power, running water, and an inside toilet. I was getting pretty comfortable driving the big bright yellow truck and was missing K for Krap less and less every day. I drove Old Yeller like she was on rails and quickly earned "Flight of the Bumblebee" status around town. The bottom line was there was no way I was getting anywhere incognito, so I figured I'd might as well just drive it from destination to destination as quickly as possible to lessen my embarrassment.

One afternoon, Dad had sent Jared and I to the neighbors' to pick up some new patio furniture they were getting rid of, it was going to go in the area of the yard where the Wee Chateau had sat for the last few years. En route I mentioned to Jared that I thought Old Yeller could make it to Canyon Creek. Jared didn't believe me for one minute, and dared me to take the back way home from the neighbors house to do a little test run on the suspension.

We were cruising through the back woods and Old Yeller was handling the rough road and mud pretty well until we got to a tight spot with deep mud and a tight corner. I stopped the truck and surveyed the situation.

"Jared, am I clear in your zip code?" I asked (given that his side of the truck was five feet away from me).

"Oh you're clear, Kayla, way clear." he responded.

"You sure?" I hollered.

"Just go! You'll make it, plenty of room!" he yelled back.

I hit the gas and started to go, the truck got stuck in the deep mud and I started rocking it from drive to reverse to get us out of the rut. Finally the tires slipped free and the next thing I know we're full speed out of the mud heading for the bend. I cranked the wheel as hard as I could, but unfortunately the steering wheel was practically as large as the Wheel of Fortune, and without power steering made driving it pretty darn close to giving the Wheel of Fortune a rip in front of Bob Barker.

I was just about to scream, "Whoo hoo!" when I felt a very hard thud and heard Jared scream like a little girl.

"OH SHIT KAYLA!" Jared yelled.

I slammed on the brakes and slapped him twice. Once for cussing and once for not realizing the truck was NOT in fact clear.

Jared was still sitting in awe on his side of the bench seat peering out the passenger window when I jumped out to survey the damage. Where was a Wee Chateau when you needed it? I nearly crapped my pants when I saw what had happened.

I'd taken out the passenger side mirror with a pine tree.

To say I was distracted was the understatement of the year. I was experiencing my first real love, and it was apparent in all areas of my life.

When I got the truck home Dad wasn't pleased, but the damage was minimal and we changed the story up enough that he was ultimately happy that Jared and I had escaped a dangerous situation with little damage, in other words, it was a good thing I hit the tree to avoid the car that was in my lane.

" Trouble" had recently told me he'd taken a job with a lumber mill up north and was going to be leaving town in a few weeks. We didn't really talk about what would happen when he left, I'm not sure I much wanted to think about it because I was head over heels, tingle in the bottom of my gut, in love with him.

He called me up one afternoon and told me a bunch of people were heading down to Canyon Creek later that night. I made arrangements to "sleep over at a friend's house" whose parents were so high on marijuana half the time that they didn't know which way was up, so that I could go out for the night and wouldn't have to worry about curfew, which was way earlier than all my friends'. I got a few other girls to ride with me to Canyon Creek in Old Yeller figuring that she'd make it just fine sans one mirror.

The night was marvelous, the sky was clear, the stars were countless and Sublime was telling everyone at the party that night about "40 ounces to Freedom." I didn't have a care in the world. My friends ended up getting rides home with various friends and guys and "Trouble" asked me if I wanted to come home with him.

Since Mom and Dad thought I was staying over at a friend's house, I'd figured it would be the perfect ending to a great night.

Around midnight we left Canyon Creek and he drove Old Yeller to his house, I guess I didn't think much about the fact that it was getting low on gas at the time; I had more important things on my mind.

Sometime after midnight, lying in his bed I had a pretty big girl decision to make. It didn't take much enticing on his part, I was excited and in love and ready. The only thing I asked him after we were done was, "The Southern Pacific pulled out on time, right?"

"Trouble" looked at me for a minute or two, and then he started laughing and said, "Yes, my Southern Pacific is equipped with airbags."

That made me laugh out loud, then I rolled over and fell asleep.

The next morning I left "Trouble's" house in the same clothes I'd worn the night before, I was running late to work, which was becoming pretty standard since I'd started dating him. When I hopped in the truck I was still trying to grasp everything that had just happened. I was also trembling, excited, nervous, scared, happy and even a little confused. I looked down at the gas and it showed a quarter tank, I'd never run it so low, but the trip to Canyon Creek had drained it. I figured the gas I had was plenty to get me to work.

I was driving at my usual "way too fast" speed when suddenly Old Yeller started puttering out. I looked down and the tank still read a quarter full. I was on a hill and was hoping I could coast down to the gas station. I was wrong.

I barely jerked Old Yeller over to the side of the road before she completely stalled.

I stood on the side of the road contemplating my choices before using a receipt to write a note. "OUT OF GAS BACK SOON" was what the paper I stuck in the windshield read, even though I had no intention of coming back for that truck.

I walked the rest of the way to work and was REALLY late by the time I got there. I still didn't care. I picked up the phone and called Mom and Dad. I left a message on the answering machine.

"Your piece of shit truck is out of gas even though it says it's got a quarter tank."

I left them the location of the truck, and they drove together once they got home with a gas can and filled it up. Actually, the truck ran empty at a quarter of a tank, small little problem that my Grandpa forgot to tell Dad about when he sold it to him.

Didn't really matter, the way Mom and Dad saw it, it was my responsibility living in a small mountain town to keep it a half a tank full at all times, and it was even MORE my responsibility to deal with problems like an adult when they came up. In other words, I shouldn't have left the truck on the side of the road for Dad to deal with, and I especially shouldn't have left it blocking someone's driveway, which I honestly did not realize at the time.

I got a ride home from work that day and contemplated not going home at all. I would have to face the music sooner or later, so I just decided to buck up and deal with it. I hadn't stepped one foot inside the trailer when Mom started in on me.

"Michaela, your father and I want to talk to you." Mom started.

"Boys, go outside for a bit please." Dad said.

Three things about this were not good; "Michaela," "Father," and "boys outside."

The fight started with the truck running out of gas, and taking responsibility for my actions and quickly turned into who knew what was best for me and my life, and it didn't take long for my "loser" boyfriend to get drug into it. They didn't think "Trouble" was good enough for me, and never would and they pretty much said that they believed all my bad decisions of late were his fault and that I should stop seeing him immediately.

Then they started rambling on about my goals and dreams and aspirations in life, and Mom launched into some big talk about not winding up pregnant at seventeen like her, which lead to an even larger fight between her and Dad. This lead to me telling Mom that I knew she never wanted me, which lead to Dad getting mad at me, which lead to me telling them I was going to run away, which lead to Mom telling me, "GO THEN."

I was a good kid, who worked two jobs and got perfect grades and helped them raised my brothers. I didn't need them telling me how to live my life. So I opted to take Mom's invitation and stormed out of the trailer and jumped in the truck, which now had a full tank of gas.

I got half-way to MarVal when I had to turn around, I'd realized in my haste I'd forgotten my purse and that running away without a purse would be difficult.

For obvious reasons my adrenaline was rushing and I was driving way too fast, which I didn't realize until after I was already half way into the corner. Next thing I know the truck was leaning hard, with two wheels in the air and the other two squealing. Wouldn't you know it, Dad happened to be coming around the bend at the exact same time, apparently chasing after me since I'd left the way I did.

From my inverted 180° angle I saw his expression through his windshield; I pulled out of the turn safely and kept on driving. I don't have to tell you that by the time we both pulled up the driveway I was grounded. Dad didn't even say a word, he just stuck out his hands. I dropped the keys to Old Yeller and told him I hated him for what he was doing.

The next day I helped Jared load the back of Old Yeller for a trip to the dump. Jared was straight ticked that I'd screwed up so badly because since I was grounded I wasn't even allowed to go to the dump (poor poor me) which meant he had to go with Mom.

The truck was loaded to the brim, both inside and out. Jared crawled inside and Mom turned the engine on, since I had been the last to drive the radio turn dial was cranked up and one of Notorious B.I.G's ladies was saying, "I like it when you call me Big Pappa." Mom immediately started acting jiggy with it and attempted to sing along. It just so happened that an old 1960's lamp we'd first used when we got power to the trailer was sitting in between Jared and Mom on the bench seat, next I thing I see is Mom putting Old

Yeller's gear shift in drive and Jared grabbing the lampshade and sticking it over his head for the dump trip. I busted up laughing, that was an incredibly creative way to ride in Old Yeller. Wish I'd thought to put some eye holes in it and driven Old Yeller that way, maybe I would have been able to slow down a little bit.

A few more glorious weeks had gone by, we were about ready to start the sheet rock on the house and I had re-earned the keys to Old Yeller. This time around I was savvy about sneaking out to see "Trouble" and was becoming incredibly more creative about ways to see him. I was living life in the moment, taking advantage of every spare minute I had; which, since I had two jobs, wasn't very many. There was only a few days left before he was supposed to leave town and I decided I would head over after work and surprise him.

Since I'd been sneaking over early in the mornings before work and late at night I knew where the hide-a-key was, so I let myself in. I'd brought pizza from Papa's Pizzeria and headed toward his room. I heard noises and probably should have taken that as a warning to leave. But my young mind never could have grasped the concept of what was happening. All those weekends and nights when I was working, he was still out having fun.

I dropped the pizza on the ground when I shoved open the door and saw his sister's best friend naked and on top of him.

"Michaela!" he yelled as I turned to run. I cried the whole way home. I was too embarrassed to tell my parents, so instead I told my brothers.

I didn't respond to even one of his myriad calls, so a few days later when he came up the driveway with his buddies I was mortified. He should have left town by now. My heart was racing, I wanted nothing to do with him, I had nothing to say. I sat inside the trailer thinking about what to do and was pretty happy when my brothers come to my rescue. My little brothers were growing up to be pretty big boys.

"Stay inside, Sis," Robert began, "Jared, come with me."

Jared picked up a two by four lying nearby and headed down the driveway with Robert. From the window above the fifth wheel where my parent's bed was I watched my little brothers handle the situation like grown men.

"Where's your sister?" "Trouble" yelled.

"She's not around, and I don't think you have any business being here," Jared said.

"I don't think that's for you to say, I need to tell her something," he finished.

"You've said enough," Robert started. "You can leave on your own, or we can carry you out."

"Your choice," Jared finished, thumping the two by four against his palm for extra emphasis.

A minute later, I watched "Trouble" and his buddies back down the driveway, and that was the last time I ever saw him. I guess Mom and Dad were right after all.

FULL GALLON OF MILK

"Kayla, head on down to Georgetown Divide Supply with Old Yeller to pick up the first round of sheetrock!" Dad yelled from somewhere behind the framed walls of the house. He was knee deep in pipes with Mom and I was just sitting there swirling around pipe glue.

"Jared!" I screamed as I fished around trying to find the keys to Old Yeller.

"Yeah?!" Jared peered up from the squirrel he had shot and killed earlier that morning.

My grandpa had been an electrician for years and had brought my grandmother up for the day to help my parents with finishing up the electrical and the plumbing. We were just about ready to begin sheetrocking the house. Nanny and Papa always brought gifts for us when they came to visit, this time Papa had brought Jared and Robert BB guns. Dad had threatened him not to shoot anything living, including each other, but they didn't listen and had shot and killed a squirrel.

They'd told them the rules, anything they shot they had to eat. I guess my brothers didn't believe that they'd actually make them go through with it, but sure enough when they brought that squirrel home, the first thing Papa did was taught Jared how to skin it. That was far more than my weak stomach could handle so I went and stuck my nose in some pipe glue. Barely twelve years old and Jared was a regular ole Grizzly Adams.

When I finally found the keys to Old Yeller, Jared was just about done grilling the squirrel.

"Come with me to pick up the sheetrock!"

"Sure thing!" Jared was jumping at the chance to get out of eating the squirrel.

"Not before you eat that squirrel you went and shot, son!" Papa hollered.

Jared and Robert fought over who would go first and then it was determined they would eat it at the same time. I told them to hold their nose.

The look on their faces was enough to make the strongest at heart vomit, but they did it. One thing was certain, they'd learned their lesson. That'd be the last time they'd use those BB guns to shoot anything they didn't plan on eating.

"Tastes like chicken!" Jared yelled. But we all knew he was full of it.

Jared and I hopped in Old Yeller and headed to get the sheetrock. Dad had been promoted over the years, from foreman to superintendent.

With the raise, and the promise of a year long salary without winter layoffs, Dad was able to put down the money we needed to purchase plumbing and electrical materials as well as the sheetrock for the house.

We lived on the same shoe-string budget that we had been for a year to pull it off, maybe even a little tighter. My jobs were covering all my expenses. I was helping out around the house and we all wanted to move into the house so badly that even the boys had taken up odd jobs around town to help out with groceries and such.

Seeing the framed house just wasn't enough for any of us, it was so close we could taste it. We could envision the full sized shower, a real bed and a full sized refrigerator, Jared loved cereal, but never got it because milk was too expensive (we even made mac and cheese with water) our fridge was barely large enough to fit a ¼ gallon of milk.

The winter was fading and we were facing the beginning of spring. The two by four's that had been drenched by the rain over the last few months were drying out. The next few weeks we spent sheetrocking the house, Dad had concocted a wooden box made out of plywood that held sheetrock mud. We would dump rolls of tape in and pull it out and it was simple enough for all of us to help.

I had started applying to universities a few months prior against the better wishes of my parents. Mom and Dad weren't prepared to let their little girl go and tried to talk me out of any university farther than Sacramento State. The concept of living in the college dorms was more than Dad could bare and he suggested I move in with my grandma (his Mom who was lonely ever since my grandpa had passed away) and attend college in Sacramento.

Mom's parents were incredibly supportive (almost demanding) of my dreams to attend university and offered to co-sign on any college loan that I might need. The selection process was hard. I knew one thing for certain, the university had to have a journalism program, and I preferred if it was as far away from Georgetown as possible. I was ready to get out of the one-horse town and see the world.

I firmly believed a college education was the only way for me to succeed in life, and my idea of succeeding was having a great career, a handsome husband and a beautiful house. Preferably somewhere near the ocean, the American Dream,

I wanted every piece of it. I knew the value of fighting for something and I knew the hard work it would take to achieve that. Nothing had been handed to me in life, and I wasn't afraid of the fact that given my parents' financial situation, if college was what I wanted, I could have it, but I'd work tooth and nail for every ounce of it.

By the time mid-spring rolled around we had fully textured and painted the house. Mom had placed the trailer up for sale, as extra motivation for us to finish up the loose ends of the house.

The day the inspector showed up and walked through the house, we all held our breath. One by one he checked off each item and finally he gave us the ok. Technically, the house was livable, and we didn't waste a minute moving everything out of the trailer and into the house. Dad disconnected all the power and water, and memories of the old tree and the water tower, and the guy showing up to hook up our phone line for the first time came flooding back.

A few days later someone showed up to look at the trailer. The trailer was certainly nothing to look at, but in four years we'd built a new life based on nothing more than love. Just like leaving any home, part of me was sad to see it go. The memories that were made changed who each of us were as individuals, and helped us grow into a single team rather than a family of five people.

The love surrounding the trailer resounded a flute in the wind and it was not lost on the potential buyer who came to look at it. Even Buddy (who had run away the year before) and Effie Lynn (who had finally passed away) had made their mark on the tiny twenty-seven foot fifth wheel.

There was a study that was conducted a few years ago, where they took different color chalk and put it on the bottom of a family's shoes. When the family came in the house they had to slip on the shoes and go about their regular business. What the study concluded was that each member of the family actually followed in the other's footsteps, and that there were zones where each family consistently congregated. And they learned that families can actually survive together in spaces much smaller than they realize.

Our family had flourished living together in two hundred square feet. At times it was difficult, at times it was sad and stressful, but in exchange we became a tightly bonded team that not even the greatest of life's troubles could break.

The man stood back from the trailer and looked in each of our eyes directly. He made a comment under his breath about it being "remarkable" and told Mom he would take it. He didn't offer her a penny less than her asking price. He paid cash, he hooked up the rig and he drove it away. That was it.

Looking at the house, which was so much nicer than the trailer it was hard to be sad…I'm pretty sure that Mom wasn't sad at all. But it was bittersweet for me.

The house was approximately 1200 square feet, my parents plan was to eventually build on and turn this half of the house into the garage. The footprint of the house was a footprint of a standard four-car garage, one side of the two-car-garage was the master bedroom for Mom and Dad and the other was split with a pony wall into two bedrooms, one for me and one for the boys to share.

There was a great room, the kitchen area that extended into the living area. We had some makeshift cabinets along the back wall of the kitchen and Mom had the basic white kitchen appliances. Dad put in a wood burning stove to keep us warm and a few steps up lead to an area with a full size washer and dryer and a bathroom which would later be a part of the final house. The floors were cement so Dad used carpet remnants to provide some soft padding under our feet. There were no doors on the rooms so we hung sheets for privacy. After living in the trailer that long a sheet hanging where a door should be felt like the privacy the President gets in the White House.

Mom had drug me around town to various yard sales with Old Yeller and had found a great deal on a bunk bed for the boys and a twin bed for me. On the way home from our umpteenth yard sale Mom stopped off at Ace Hardware.

Just before we walked in she told me I could pick out a paint color for my room. It was the first time Mom and I had done something for the house that was what I considered feminine. Mom was always an excellent interior decorator, and even with the horrible trailer situation she had managed to make it look nice, sewing a cabin-flannel patterned slip covers for the seat pads in the trailer and putting some wall paper on the inside to make it feel cozier. I was excited to be a part of the decorating of the house, even if it was only the paint in my room.

It had been so long since I'd had a room of my own. The last house we lived in I had peach walls, and Mom and Nanny had painted the boys' room powder blue with Charlie Brown characters all over the walls.

I stood looking at all the choices available and finally selected a mint green. It felt light and bright and full of life compared to the dark blues, reds and bland beiges.

Since Mom and I were going to be spending the better half of the day deal shopping for basic furniture needs for the house Mom had given the boys $100 cash to go to the grocery store and buy groceries to fill the refrigerator.

Mom hollered at the boys to help us come unload Old Yeller but they didn't come out of the house. We gathered up the first load and carried it inside. Mom was mortified when she saw what Jared and Robert had done. They were literally sitting on the floor in the living room with a massive stainless steel bowl in front of them; they were surrounded by two gallons of milk and six cereal boxes, Fruit Loops, Lucky Charms, Fruity Pebbles, Cocoa Puffs, Captain Crunch and Cheerios.

They had used the entire $100 to purchase cereal and milk and absolutely nothing else. The other four gallons of milk they'd purchased were in the full size refrigerator. The boys knew what their priority was, so the rest of us were either going to have to join in on the cereal party, or starve for the rest of the week.

It wasn't that the boys weren't mature enough to handle the task; it wasn't that they didn't understand the value of the dollar because all three of us knew it all too well, it was that they wanted to celebrate and were far too young to purchase champagne.

That night when Dad got home Mom walked him around the house showing him all the things we'd picked up, and all the money we'd saved, all the negotiating we'd done and he was proud of what Mom had been able to accomplish on such a tight budget.

Then she announced that we were having Breakfast for Dinner.

"Oh that sounds great, Hun!" Dad exclaimed as he looked around.

"Yeah, courtesy of the boys, they did the shopping today." Mom threw the boys a disapproving look.

Dad immediately knew from the look on my mother's face, and the fact there was no smell of bacon grease wafting through the air, that our dinner would not be something you'd find on the menu at the Waffle Barn.

We could eat cereal for a year, I didn't care, we were finally living in a real house, with real walls and a real shower, and lots of space to just sit on the floor and spread out and for once I wasn't embarrassed to have people over.

My prom was quickly approaching and I was quite pleased with my date. I had met him a few weeks before, he had just gotten out of the Marine Corps and moved back home to Georgetown. His younger sister was in my class, and I'd always thought he was quite good looking. He was tall, about 6'3, lean, muscular and mature, about four years older than me, and I found that incredibly attractive.

Mom stuck the last bobby pin in my hair and I walked out of the house to greet him. He was a breath of fresh air standing there in his Dress Blues. I smiled while my parents and grandparents snapped photographs and couldn't help but chuckle, ironically there was no K for Krap car, there was no Wee Chateau, and no trailer as I had envisioned my prom would be years before. Just a beautiful Marine, holding a gorgeous corsage made of red, white and blue flowers.

I had chosen a navy dress that Mom and I picked out at an antique (second hand) store in Auburn. I was blessed with "birthin hips" as Mom called them, which I really didn't care for or want, but along with her bottom half curves, I'd also gotten her upper half curves. When I stepped out of the fitting room I knew it was just perfect. An A-line gown that swept up around my neck and pinned in the back, it hugged me tightly in all the right places.

The pain that "Trouble" had caused was a distant memory and I was proud to be on this Marine's arm tonight. We said goodbye to my parents and Dad gave him the standard "hurt her and I'll kill you." I waved to my little brothers, Mom was delighted with the way my makeup and hair had turned out and my grandparents were beaming, everyone was so proud.

He opened my door and helped me into his truck and then we headed for the canyon. Prom was being held at a fancy hotel in the city. As I looked over the lapels on his suit jacket I imagined all the neat things he'd experienced in the military. We began to talk about my plans for after high school and I shared with him my biggest hope in life. I'd applied to Pepperdine University in Malibu, home to one of the best journalism programs in the State.

He chuckled a bit and reiterated that I'd always been a firecracker, taking life on headfirst, and then questioned how I planned to pay for it. I shared with him that the only way I'd be going was if I could go for an in person interview because I'd heard from my school counselor it was the only way they'd offer a scholarship.

When we arrived at the hotel there was another reception happening, the building was surrounded by people in business suits, drinking cocktails and snacking on appetizers that looked far too small to satisfy even a child's appetite. I couldn't help but find the whole thing exciting.

Later that evening we danced to Chris De Burgh's "Lady In Red," and as I closed my eyes to let him lead I imagined myself on the other side of the ballroom divider, wearing a black suit, attending some journalism gala and devouring fancy snacks.

ROCK CRAWLING

It's called Rock Crawling. It's what we do up in the sticks for fun. And fun does not begin to describe it. It's absolutely riveting, exciting, daring, hysterical, dirty and challenging entertainment, especially for a bunch of hillbilly's. "City Slickers" fork out big money to Jeep Jamboree to experience the back mountain soul searching trip from Georgetown to Lake Tahoe every summer.

For locals, the challenge begins with building the best Rock Crawler imaginable. This process starts when an individual decides whether their loyalties lie with Toyota or Jeep. The rivalry is comparable to the 49'ers versus the Raiders, the Hatfield's versus the McCoy's, or Coke versus Pepsi.

Then the mission to create the baddest four wheel drive machine begins. Typically a perfectly horrendous stock Toyota or Jeep is purchased from the junk yard and then destroyed even further. The chassis is reinforced, suspension spring or coils are enhanced, gears and lockers are installed so you have 24/7 positive traction on the front and rear tires. Extreme oversize wheels with aggressive tread patterns are swapped for stock tires, gear ratio is tuned down, the torque is increased and dual transfer cases double the four-wheel drive capabilities in low range. Meaning literally, the vehicle can be kicked into first gear, the driver can get out for a bathroom break, pop open a beer and the crawler will still be chugging along at one mile an hour on its own without stalling. Finally a roll cage and seats with five point harnesses are added for safety.

The Rock Crawlers meet at Loon Lake, which is where the road gets technical.

The trail is just over seventeen miles from Georgetown to Lake Tahoe through El Dorado National Forest and will take an experienced crawler seven to eight hours. Its dirt and mud, its gorgeous back mountain trails and terrifying sheer granite cliffs. Half way into the trail is Rubicon Springs, the most peaceful, serene area of the National Forest. There is also a campground, and in the middle of the summer, there is plenty of beer and good food.

My first trip into Rubicon Springs was in a helicopter owned and operated by Jeep Jamboree (who had sponsored me in the Miss El Dorado Pageant), my second trip was in one of the brand new TJ's off the production line from Chrysler and most trips following were in well built CJ's.

This trip was in a 1949 Willy's, built by my Marine boyfriend, that frankly I had zero faith in. I met up with him at Loon Lake; our crew was sixteen deep and consisted of a dangerous combination of some of the best crawlers in Georgetown, which meant the day would include a bunch of boys trying to show off their 4-wheelin' skills, with ego's flying higher than kites in the summer.

Everything was going well on the trail until we hit the Sluice Box. The Sluice Box is nicknamed such due to the geography of the slope and the way the trail washes out, it's also the most difficult part of the trail. The rain and snowmelt change it every year, which means, no matter how many times you've crawled the Rubicon, each year you never know what to expect when you get to the Sluice.

I'd be doing a lot of riding as passenger, and a little bit of driving, and had done the trail enough times to know his Jeep was in no condition to tackle the Sluice. I suggested he go around, which only fired up his ego. After a bit of bickering he told me that if I didn't want to ride the Sluice, I'd need to hop out and walk it because he was tackling it either way. I am no idiot, and decided to get out plus I was tired of arguing, I figured if he was going to fail best he do it without me in the co-pilot seat.

It was a good thing I did. He had way too much speed as he hit the deepest part of the Sluice, he was less than half way through before he high-sided on a slab of granite and busted his axle.

The guys spent a few hours attempting to fix the crawler, but it had no hope. Finally some friends offered to tow the Jeep back to Loon Lake. Rest assured, getting towed while sitting in any vehicle is not fun, but let me tell you, getting towed through the dirt and the mud in a 4wd with nearly no suspension and a busted axle while getting slammed over the rocks is complete torture. Literally, every bone in my body was being jarred. I could not hear myself think, and the Marine and I had completely had it out (arguing over his ego). We ended up breaking up somewhere between Spider and Loon Lakes. By the time I got home I had dirt in every orifice and crevasse on my body and I was in dire need of a shower.

The Marine screamed something like "Good Riddance" as I jumped out of his Willy's and I flipped him off as I stormed up the driveway for the shower. From the days in the trailer we had gotten used to leaving the door unlocked during the shower in case someone needed to use the bathroom. I heard a knock on the door immediately after I stepped in the shower and pulled the shower curtain.

"Sis you covered up?" Mom asked. "Why are you home so early, thought you were going to the Rubicon?"

"I don't want to talk about it. The Marine and I broke up because of his stupid Jeep."

"Oh no, can I come in?" she asked

She'd just gotten home from work, I figured she had to pee and it was going to take me awhile to get all this dirt off me.

"Come in." I replied.

There was a lot of excitement in her voice as she began to speak, "You got a letter in the mail from Pepperdine today."

"Is it small, or large?" I asked her.

"It's small!" she exclaimed. Simultaneously I could hear her begin to trickle in the toilet and tear open the envelope. I went from being angry to incredibly sad as I watched the water flow off my body and create a brown swirl of mud in the bottom of the shower.

"Mom…" I tried to interrupt. But she'd already started.

"We thank you for taking the time to apply to Pepperdine University School of Journalism, we regret to inform…" her voice trailed off.

I began sobbing.

"I'm so, so sorry, Sis." Mom offered as she flushed the toilet.

"Just go." I said.

I heard the door close and I crouched to the bottom of the shower, trying to stop the pain in my stomach. Just like I'd learned years before, as long as I was in the shower, the tears just washed away without evidence. Everything I'd planned, everything I'd hoped for was all for not. I began to fear I would never get out of the small town.

Mom and Dad couldn't afford to send me to college and I had no back up plan. I was stuck in the Sluice with a busted axle. My dream was a four year university and that was out the window.

When Dad came home that night he had a talk with me. "Look, it's just like rock crawling," he started.

I was beyond depressed and didn't want to hear a bit of what he had to say.

"Sometimes the terrain gets tough, no matter how much we try to plan, or how well we think we've done we get stuck, and it's not up to us, we can't control it. So we kick it in four low, weigh the options and we rock crawl," he finished.

The problem was, as usual, what Dad said made sense.

Shortly after that I took a job off the hill working for Gottshalks. I figured I could go to the two year college and get the basic classes out of the way, and with excellent grades I could transfer to the university of my choice.

It was there that I met my future husband. I'll never forget the day. I was working in the children's department and he was working in the men's department. I'd been working there all of two days, and desperately needed help with a product return. He was the only one around.

I was seventeen and our relationship was a whirlwind tour of young love. I had been living in pure romantic bliss for three months, when the package arrived.

I had been attending day classes at the junior college and working the night shift at Gottshalks. When I got home after a long week the house was empty, and dark. There was a hand written note resting on top of an eight and half by eleven envelope, "Sis, took the boys to dinner, love Mom and Dad."

I gently pushed the note to the side to reveal:
Pacific Lutheran University
School of Mass Communications
Tacoma, WA

I sat down, took a deep breath and opened it up. "Dear Ms. Jacques, we are sorry that your application was misplaced during the early application process, but after reviewing your package would like to extend an invitation to the School of Mass Communications at PLU…" the letter trailed on and concluded with, "Based upon your excellent grades and journalism experience, we'd like to extend a scholarship of $12,000 per year…"

I was getting the hell out of dodge! I did the chicken dance meets victory dance around the kitchen for a good fifteen minutes. That's when the phone rang.

"HELLO?!" I screamed at whoever was on the other end.

It was my future husband. Suddenly my excitement slid into confusion. I hadn't given any thought to what would come of him and I. I spent a few days weighing my options, but at the end of the day I was going to Washington, the first step in chasing the American Dream, a college education.

The final hours before I left him we sat in the driveway talking about the past, and wondering about our future. George Strait's, "She'll leave you with a smile" was quietly trickling from the radio in his car.

We kissed and let it linger and then I opened the door and stepped out, I felt the pine needles crunch under my boots as he jumped out of the car and ran over to embrace me one last time. I wiped away my first tear as I watched him pull down the driveway.

Dad had loaded up the carrier on top of the car and as I crawled in the backseat I took one last look around and waved, it was bittersweet. Mom got in the front seat and the three of us headed north on Interstate 5. Mom said somewhere between Chico and Eureka I cried myself to sleep. We pulled into the parking lot of the University and it was obvious Dad had been crying too. Rumor has it that he cried from the California border to the Washington state line.

When we got to the University, I began the registration process and got the keys to my new dorm. Everything was exactly as I expected it would be, except the realization was hitting me that Mom and Dad would be leaving soon, and I would be incredibly alone, and far from everyone and everything I knew. Tacoma was a small town, but it was no where near as tiny as Georgetown.

We put the finishing touches on my dorm room…and as I walked them to the car, just before they drove away Dad turned and held me in a tight hug, the way he used to do when I was a little girl and he began to choke up he said, "Sis?"

"Yeah, Dad?" I asked as I tried to stay strong.

"You'll come home and bless us with your presence right?"

I lost it. My life had changed, I was officially no longer the baby girl, I was a grown woman, out on her own. I was living in the ellipsis, the dot dot dot, pause in speech or intentionally omitted word, trailing off into silence.

"Jeez, Dad," was all I could muster out as I wiped my tears.

PART II

HAPPINESS = LOVE + EVERYTHING MINUS EVERYTHING

ONE WAY TICKET

For the first time in my life, I was hogtied laying in the mud at negative zero and I had absolutely no control over what had happened. It was as if I watched the whole thing from someone else's body. During the forty-five second ride down the escalator my quote unquote accomplishments flashed before my eyes; a college education paid for exclusively by yours truly, a successful career in marketing, not one- but two profitable real estate transactions by the age of twenty-six, a house with a white picket fence and an ocean view, a faithful husband, a retired racing greyhound named Rio and pound kitty wild Bengal cat named Dash shattered into pieces. The American Dream, left somewhere in the front seat of my car in San Diego. The bottom line is I was a grown woman and I was running home to Mom and Dad.

The worst part was that I had disappointed them, because ten years earlier they thought they armed me with the strength to go out into the world and stand up for myself.

After a cold lonely night in a hotel room in San Diego I found myself standing at the Southwest Airlines ticket counter, I was looking for a one-way ticket to Georgetown. My worst nightmare and my greatest relief wrapped up in a one hour flight from San Diego to Sacramento Airport.

As I sat uncomfortably in the very first row of the plane I realized that not even my iPod could drown out the sound of my brain, which was quite literally thumping over and over with "your life as you know it is over." I felt like the world's biggest failure. I was scared, and confused and terrified.

I'd built an amazing life and a strong marriage; he truly was a wonderful man, except for his temper.

And now, at twenty-seven, I was becoming a statistic. I wasn't strong enough to beat the odds, I wasn't good enough or smart enough to fix our marriage. I was just about to lose everything. I was a quitter.

As I rode the escalator down to baggage claim at the Sacramento Metropolitan Airport I saw my parents waiting at the bottom. The words escaped my mouth and floated into the air surrounding the escalator, "Well I guess my brother doesn't have to feel like the family eff up now."

But in this moment my parents put that aside and as I stepped my first toe off the escalator they began to cry with me, I guess no matter how old or independent you become you are always their little girl.

THE PHONE CALL

It is a forty-five minute car ride from Sacramento to Georgetown. As Dad pulled the car onto Interstate 5, the speeding highway and the rain caused my mind to replay the events of the night before as if they had just happened.

Through my tears I watched as my husband opened the driver door and began to run. My friend jumped out of the backseat and made a split second decision, chase after my husband or take care of me. He ripped open my door and lifted me out; I was inconsolable, hysterical and shaking. As he carried me kicking and screaming to his truck he yelled, "How long Michaela? How long has this been going on?"

He tossed me like a ragdoll into his truck, buckled my seatbelt and slammed the door. He'd had a few drinks like the rest of us and I remember I was terrified, it was hailing now, and he was speeding. He thrust his cell phone into my palm.

"CALL YOUR DAD. RIGHT NOW." He demanded.

"Please, just give me a minute, please," I sobbed.

"Tell me the number right now," he said as he began to pull up the keypad on his phone. Eventually I caved and he dialed the number. As the phone began to ring he shoved it to my ear and said, "Tell them right now, or I will."

"Dad," I started.

"Sis, what's going on it's late?" Dad asked nervously.

As I began to explain I heard Mom interject, "Tom, what the hell is going on?"

Mom's voice from the background provided a visual of the look on my father's face. And immediately after my answer was the sound of a father's heart breaking in two.

In a matter of minutes my future was stolen, my heart was crushed, my head was confused. There would be no more cover-ups, no more begging for mercy, no more empty promises and no more lies. If only for the minor shred of dignity I had left there would be no turning back. He pulled the truck into the nearest Marriott and checked me in. I need a place to lie down, even though I wouldn't be sleeping.

GUACAMOLE WON'T FIX IT

As I watched the barren fields of the outskirts of Sacramento become the oak trees of Granite Bay I hoped that if I sobbed silently and took quiet breaths that perhaps my parents would forget I was in the backseat at all. Every now and then I'd hear one of them begin to ask a question, but they could not find the words. Their silence was valued because I was in no position to begin explaining, I couldn't even comprehend it myself.

From the look of my jeans hanging loosely off my hips and protruding collar bone my parents figured I hadn't been eating so they pulled over for some Mexican food well knowing guacamole is not something I can typically resist. Dad sat across from me in the booth and Mom sat next to me. They ate while I broke the flimsy chips into three-thousand pieces and waited for me to speak.

I didn't have anything to say, until I saw the hurt in Dad's eyes. All I could muster up was, "I'm so sorry, Dad." Right then Mom put her fork down, dropped her head in her hands and cried so hard she choked.

There was a long silence while I tried to dry my tears but the napkin was cheap and crumbled into a bazillion pieces. Maybe going out to eat wasn't such a good idea.

All I wanted to do was sink underneath the table and meld into a puddle of colors matching the tile mosaic on the floor, or run as far away as humanly possible and hide, because even guacamole couldn't fix this.

We pulled up the driveway in silence, as I stepped out of the car I felt the crunching of the pine needles and took my first deep breath. I was home. I was safe, and Georgetown was just about as far away from civilization as any place I could dream up. As Dad turned to head down the hallway he mentioned that they had cleaned out the spare bedroom and the office so I could stay as long as I needed to clear my head. They also added that they'd leave me alone until I sorted through it, which I doubted, but regardless I needed to figure out what to do next.

My pride stung like I'd walked into a hornets nest and I felt a mad desire to somehow justify it all. What I would learn is that justifying ones actions to the world only requires a couple of breaths, or a few strokes on the keyboard.

Justifying to oneself requires reflection.

THE FINAL NIGHT

As I laid in the spare bed at my parent's house I thought about the moments that lead up to those final three minutes in the car. Until that moment, it had only been between me and my soul, and no one else.

The San Diego Chargers had lost the big game. It was raining and a group of us wound up at the local dive bar to drink our sorrows away. My inhibitions were low and my ability to hide the truth was becoming much more difficult.

We stumbled to the closest friend's house we could find and spent quite a bit of time trying to sober up. It wasn't until we left the house that I realized my purse was missing.

We'd gone back to the bar with a few friends, checked in dumpsters and asked the barfly's. No one had seen it, the purse was no where to be found. I started to sober up quickly when I realized I had no wallet, no keys, no cell phone and that literally my entire life was in that purse. Our house was only a few blocks from the bar and the thief could very well be there robbing us using the address on my drivers license.

My husband was doing nothing to help. We were supposed to be a team, but he was too livid and busy calling me a sloppy drunk to actually help rectify the situation.

I can't say I didn't see it coming, I'd been enduring it long enough to know when the demon was awake, as the fight over my lost purse worsened I became nervous, but I never fathomed he'd do anything in front of our friends. It wasn't until his fist was brushing the bottom of my chin that I screamed.

It was too late.

I didn't yell out in pain, I screamed in agony. With the crack of my jaw, went my right to keep it hidden. The rug was tossed upside down and all the truths were exposed.

OPERATION SHOVEL DIRT

I woke up in my parent's eerily familiar yet uncomfortable spare bedroom, the last thirty-six hours had been a whirlwind and in my maniacal packing I had forgotten pajamas, so I was wearing one of Dad's bright orange Caltrans esq t-shirts. I had also forgotten to silence the ringer on my cell phone before bed and the continual beeps and chimes almost created a song as the emails and texts came flooding in. Clearly the rumors had started. No one knew where I was, and everyone was concerned, but I wasn't responding. I laid in bed wishing I'd had some Roofies to wipe out the last two days of my life.

I heard the sound of two trucks pulling up the driveway and I crawled deeper under the sheets.

"Get up, Sis!" Robert yelled as he bust through the door to the spare bedroom.

Jared was tailing behind him and yanked the sheets off. "What's the deal, Kayla? Get up."

"Look, I just want to lay here and die okay?" I said with my lips crammed face down in the jersey knit sheets.

"I bet, but guess what? It's not going to happen," Jared started.

I felt their eyes beating down on my back and I finally rolled over to expose my sleep deprived face, baggy eyes and the red mark across my jaw.

"Whoa," Robert began, "look, if you wanted to have the shit kicked outta you, you should have just come home, we'da done it for you."

The smell of sourdough toast was wafting in from the kitchen and honestly after two straight days of not eating, I was pretty hungry. I begrudgingly got out of bed and followed my brothers to the kitchen. Dad brought the toast, tomatoes and salt shaker over to the table and the four of us sat down to eat.

We sat there in silence for the first few minutes when Robert finally began. "Look, Jared and I talked about this, we're going to fly down there this weekend and fix this the old fashioned way."

"Georgetown Justice," Dad added.

My brothers were having a hard time, an almost impossible time. Even though I was the big Sis, the rule was we looked out for one another, always. I'd let them down too.

"Robert, that's fucking ridiculous. You don't even understand." I said angry at his stupid suggestion of fixing an anger problem with more anger.

"Oh we understand plenty; dude deserves to get his ass kicked." Jared interjected.

The conversation was getting heated as my brothers struggled to make sense of it in their mind. Dad finally broke it up, "Jared. Robert. There's two shovels under the house, go get them out, your sister has clearly lost sight of her roots. We'll help shovel dirt, but she's got to sort through this on her own. Let her be, she's here to clear her head. She'll figure it out."

Thus was the beginning of "Operation Shovel Dirt to Show Kayla Her Roots" and with that the entire family including old friends congregated at the house.

THE LIST

I picked up my plate and stood up from the table, I paused long enough to get a good look at the expressions on my Dad and brother's faces, and then I walked to the office and called Sarita, our marriage family therapist down in San Diego. I explained to her in grave detail what happened, and what I'd been hiding for quite sometime.

"Oh, Michaela, this changes a lot," Sarita started, "If you plan to stay in Northern California awhile we can do sessions over the phone."

That was the moment my first solo therapy session with Sarita began. An hour later Dad rounded the corner to the office as I was hanging up the phone.

"I overheard you talking with your therapist," Dad started. "You are going to go through a lot while you sort through this, and no one can make this decision for you."

"I know, Dad, it's just that, it's just that I wonder how I'll ever make the right decision and live with it," I told him.

If there ever were the perfect combination of logic and emotion, it's my father. He pondered that for a moment, "Well, Sis, why don't you write down a list of what makes your perfect partner..."

"Dad, that's ridiculous..." I began.

"Hear me out, and make a list of what you wanted in life when you left here ten years ago, and who you are today. Ask yourself if you are who you want to be, or if you can become who you wish with the current path you are walking, the decision is up to you."

The idea seemed incredibly silly, but I went with it. He told me to tuck away the list, that someday I would need it.

HOW FAR IS HALF WAY?

Someday turned out to be a few times a day, because a few times a day my mind ended up spinning like a tornado. The distance from my husband made it more difficult, not less difficult to sort through the heart and mind struggle. When my heart ached, my mind was clear and when my mind was discombobulated, my heart was relieved. That's when I'd pull out the list. There was one blaring line on that list that kept jumping out at me.

I realized staring at that line in my own handwriting that even Sarita didn't know he was abusing me, although she was savvy enough to know that something about him petrified me. She knew that the counseling was worsening the situation and one night she called him out, "Your wife has one foot out the door, and I need to know where you stand."

To that he replied, "Well...I'm not coming more than half way."

When we left counseling that night we had planned to go to Fidel's Mexican Restaurant in Solana Beach. It was my favorite, especially their guacamole. Therapy had been awful, it wasn't Sarita, she was fantastic, it was that when we left her office things got worse. It was like one of those wounds that need to heal from the inside out, the kind where you have to keep ripping the scab off so it heals the right way...and each hour on her couch we spent tearing off the scab and we left her office with an open wound and a scab dangling. Then I'd spend the next few nights watching it bleed, wondering if it would heal before it was too late.

I asked him if maybe we could go on an after-counseling date, like a reward for our punishment. Fidel's was in North county, a mile or so from our therapist, and since we lived close to downtown San Diego, Fidel's really was a treat.

We backed out of her complex and started down the street toward the red light.

"Right or left?"

"Um, well, Fidel's is in Solana Beach and that's north of Del Mar, so..."

"The light is fucking green Michaela. Right or left?"

"Um, left, no I meant right, right – north."

"IT'S TOO LATE!" he yelled.

And then we were speeding down the Coast Highway the opposite direction of Fidel's and lost.

"We can U-turn," I pleaded.

"No, you should have thought about pulling directions when you planned the brilliant date night."

"I tried to tell you turn right but..."

"Look, I don't want to go on a date night. I don't want to be in this car with you, I just want to get home."

"So that's how it is? You don't really care? Sarita is right isn't she? She asked you. She asked you straight out tonight and you told her you were only coming half way. Half way really? Because our entire marriage I've been pulling both of us, and now that I need you to stop and work on you - and SHE DOESN'T EVEN KNOW what goes on with your temper- you look her straight in the face and say you're only coming half way?"

"There is NOTHING good coming of counseling, there is nothing good coming of THIS, your stupid idea at salvation."

"This isn't fair. You can't do this to ME."

The fight worsened quickly and we both said things we shouldn't have. We were traveling about 45mph on the dark empty Coast Highway when he locked up the brakes.

I felt the seatbelt jerk tight against my chest and I felt my head hit the passenger window as the SUV rocked side to side and came to a skidding halt in the middle of the road.

By the time the car came to a stop the seatbelt was choking me. When I found my breath I looked over at him and thought of Rio and Dash at home alone, waiting for us to return. I thought of my family and my friends and the man in the driver's seat that I used to know.

Calmly and quietly and with the strength afforded my heart from the counseling session just minutes before I looked at him and said, "Look, if you want to kill something, kill yourself. I'm getting out of this car; you have no right to take my life too."

In seconds I had unbuckled the seatbelt and opened the door, ten miles from home and I'd rather walk. And just as my foot hit the pavement he gunned the engine. The door whipped open with the acceleration and I held on tight while pulling myself back into the seat. I screamed at him to please stop the car, but he sped up.

After what felt like an eternity I was safe in the car again with the door shut, and I stayed silent until he pulled in the driveway, my little stunt had really pissed him off and he finished the fight he started in the dark shadows of our living room. Curled in the corner Rio came over and licked my tears and I held her as tightly as I could. Who was he, and what had I done?

The situation was getting worse and worse by the day. With each counseling session we attended I came home and prepared for what would be 'the worst night of my life,' every night.

INDY & JAVA

I sat on the couch staring into the vast empty living room of my parent's home. Days had gone by, though I wasn't sure how many. Max, my parent's Boston bull terrier, came over and jumped in my lap to offer me some companionship. I sat there alone on the couch petting Max thinking about Rio and Dash who I'd abandoned back in San Diego with the rest of my life. The sinking feeling of loss in the pit of my stomach sent my mind back a year or two. Back to Indy and Java, the two kittens my husband and I adopted when we were just kids ourselves, shortly after we moved into our first apartment. Indy and Java had both died tragically only a year before, six weeks apart.

About six months after we started dating, we were living together, both working full time and taking eighteen units a semester at San Jose State University. Living together made financial sense, because the Silicon Valley was so ridiculously over priced that the math on the dorms made the apartment seem like a great deal. Something was missing, and so in 1999 I talked my husband into letting us adopt a six-week-old kitten.

My husband named him Indiana Jones, Indy for short, after watching the trilogy, and there was no question about the fact that Indy took a better liking to him. Indy was our laughter, he was our happiness, and with our busy schedules he was lonely. So a year later we adopted six-week-old Java. Even though they were a year apart, they grew up as a bonded pair and were raised as our children.

In mid-2005 just three months before Indy's sixth birthday he was diagnosed with renal failure, cancer they thought. It was caught at the final stage, because CRF does not show its ugly head until the kidneys are half gone. They gave him eight weeks to live.

I wasn't about to settle for that and kicked a treatment plan into high gear. For nine months, with Excel spreadsheets tracking his intake and output, special food and extra attention we kept him alive and living happy. Working from home gave me the opportunity to take care of him in the way an in-home nurse cares for a hospice patient. It also meant I never got the opportunity to escape the brutality of watching him slowly die while my husband got to leave for work every day.

Then came March 23, 2006, the day I decided that Indy should no longer suffer.

I was sitting at the dining table waiting for my husband to get home. Indy had lost over half of his body weight, he was frail, he was having troubles urinating and he could no longer make it up the stairs. He had spent the whole day hidden in the back of the carrier he was in from an earlier trip to the vets office. Java crawled into the carrier to join him.

The minute my husband walked in I told him that I couldn't watch Indy suffer anymore. Watching the vet leave the room as Indy laid there twitching sent me into a very dark place. I loathed God for delivering such an evil decision to my heart and I hated that the vet didn't give him enough of the injection the first time. I had been petting Indy and by the time she made it back with the second needle I'd forgotten I wasn't supposed to have my hand where it was. I felt his heart stop and in this moment I wished on my life I could take my decision back.

My husband didn't have any way of containing his anger but from that moment on there was no stopping him, I had killed his son in the most despicable way, not one lethal injection, but two.

I knew home was the last place I wanted to be but I knew Java was waiting. Every night he slept tucked under my arm, and I knew without his brother he needed me more now than ever before.

During the next six weeks, Java got very ill and vet after vet couldn't diagnosis his ailment. One night after a grocery shopping trip, I came home to find Java tucked away in the closet, in the exact same spot Indy had laid in the last few days of his life.

Gut instinct told me something was fatally wrong and I rushed him to the ER. Oxygen incubators, blood transfusions, forty-eight hours and $7,000 later my husband begged me to let him go. There was no way I could kill him, not after the way Indy had died.

Just thirty minutes after we learned that Java had started regenerating his own blood cells he went into cardiac arrest and died on the table. A necropsy would show us that Java had disseminated intravascular coagulation or total organ failure over the loss of his bonded sibling Indy, and had any of the vets just prescribed some anti-depressants, he might have lived.

While just weeks earlier I'd begged God never to give me the right to make the decision on life again; I cursed him for taking Java's.

DOES IT GET BETTER?

Nothing can describe the rage I endured the night that Java died. It was like nothing I'd ever seen, but I was guilty of killing the boys and inconsolable. My heart was so damaged that no amount of physical pain could cut deep enough. And by comparison what he was doing didn't seem that bad.

I had lost both of my children, six weeks apart, both at six years old. My husband detested me for holding onto Java as long as I did, and each week for two months I was reminded of my choices with an $800 payment to the credit card referenced as "Java Death."

He couldn't offer more than abuse as consolation for my depression; because it was the only way he knew how to handle his own. Each day, even his minor bouts of anger slowly began to shut down each ventricle of my heart emotionally.

Rather than beg him to stop, or attempt to defend myself or even fight back, I just took it.

While I'd been able to cope with it on a much less frequent basis for years prior I was quickly becoming completely incapable of loving him any more. When the downward spiral worsened I stuck around simply because no matter how much pain it brought nothing could hurt worse inside than the thought of literally losing everything I'd known for the last ten years, no matter how miserable I was.

It wasn't long before the lack of love became hatred and I turned cold.

WHO, WHAT, WHERE, WHEN, WHY

I'd spent two weeks in Georgetown and I still didn't have any clarity. It was lightly snowing; and I had been waiting for Mom and Dad to get home from work when all of a sudden the crunching silencing sound of losing electricity came over the house. Electronics gave one final beep of life as they kicked into back up mode and suddenly my mind went to a different place.

How could a smart, tough, educated girl like me wind up in this situation? What were my friends back in San Diego saying about our perceived perfect marriage? How could I ever face my life across the other end of the state?

What would staying with my husband say about my strength as a person? What would leaving mean for my intuition and my judgment of character? What would people think when they saw the broken down me, living in abusive relationship. What would they say about a person who couldn't stand up to her husband, couldn't help him, and had resorted to an expensive therapist? What would become of my life, the house, our finances, Rio and Dash? What would become of him, and what would become of me? Ten years of being in a committed relationship meant that I'd missed the critical dating years, and well into my late 20's I would suddenly be single.

If I stayed what would I have left, and if I left him, what would remain? The door knob turned and Mom walked in.

"Did we lose power?" she asked.

"If I walk, I lose it all for nothing," I said.

"If you stay, you've lost yourself, there's nothing left after that," she added.

"If I go I give up hope," I replied.

"If you stay you give up your dreams," she responded.

"If I stay we could have a fighting chance," I begged.

"If you leave, you get a second chance. You only get one life, ask yourself if this is what it's supposed to be," she argued.

"I just want someone else to tell me," I said.

"Sorry, you have to decide that for yourself," she said.

Later that evening the boys showed up and Dad had set up the space heaters to keep us all warm. We sat around to the light of a kerosene lantern and I wondered how I had lost myself. I wondered how he was able to hurt me, when I begged him to get control. I wondered if I'd ever find the answers.

Not having any electricity for the next few days forced us to resort to a life similar to the one we lived in the trailer; we played cards, cooked outside over a fire in the cold, we sat and told hilarious stories of the good ole days and we went bowling at the cheapest lanes in town. They made me laugh, they made me cry, and when I was too devastated to find the strength to get off the couch they took me snow-wheeling which made me feel seventeen again. I stopped thinking and just started living, without my husband. I was surprised at who I could be.

It was very early in the morning when the electronics in the house hummed back to life. I dredged into the office and immediately clicked on the Internet and went to my social networking page; it was the first time I logged on in weeks. I slowly deleted every single photo, leaving only three: me, Rio and Dash. I changed my song, my headline and my mood to let my friends know I was alive then I picked up the phone and called Dad who was already at work.

"I've made a decision. I'm ready to go back."

THE DECISION

I pulled out the list Dad had suggested I create and I confirmed what I had always known; there was more in life than this.

I had arrived in Georgetown a confused, broken down skeleton of a person, who kept right on smiling, firmly believing that strong women don't show their weakness and they don't admit fault, and they don't walk away from their marriage, or they've failed.

I had been living the "American dream" at any cost including sacrificing myself. The worse things became the more hype I created surrounding our perfect marriage. I threw dinner parties, was active in the community, I decorated and redecorated the house, I excelled at work. All things that on the surface made it appear like I had succeeded, but underneath the layers of my "life" was a girl who at the core of her being was weak.

Intrinsically we were different people, and someday he might be able to change, but never with me, even if he could I didn't like who he'd become. Somewhere along the road of achieving the American Dream I'd lost myself and I didn't want to waste another moment getting me back.

I had no idea how long or painful the journey I was about to choose would be, but when I left Georgetown that bitter cold winter, something told me I was making the right decision.

MY FIRST ONLINE BLOG
DECEMBER 31, 2007
I AINT SETTLIN

Synonyms or near-synonyms of self-esteem include:

- self-worth
- self-regard
- self-respect

As first defined by Nathaniel Branden in 1969: "…the experience of being competent to cope with the basic challenges of life and being worthy of happiness."

And includes the following property: Self-esteem as a basic human need, i.e.,"…it makes an essential contribution to the life process," "…is indispensable to normal and healthy self-development, and has a value for survival."

As I stare in the mirror the person looking back is confident. Sure of absolutely nothing, but aware that regardless of what life delivers, if only for my upbringing, I will be okay. As I walk down the street I stand tall, full of courage, and proud of the fact that I have the biggest heart.

I also have a heavy heart... this year...my challenge is finding the strength to truly believe what I already know.

I face this scary world over, anew- with the heart of the seventeen year old child I was, but weighted with years of young love lessons. My dog, Rio, as my testament, I will be okay. Every day I see myself in her. This little girl, a greyhound on the race track who didn't know any better. She did what she was told without question, she aimed to please and fell short, she was beaten down, tested to the nth degree and ran as hard and as fast as she could until she collapsed, left panting - grasping for any breath of air.

As I look at her now, I see a beautiful lady full of personality who is confident in her abilities to receive the respect she should have always had. She is surrounded by people who love her more than she could imagine. People who, simply because they love her, want to help her find her way in this world. People that no longer take advantage of her strength and beautiful heart. People who, because they see her loving soul want to genuinely help her along.

Somehow, through her years of grief and now her new found happiness she manages to go out to the same ugly world she trudged through and help others, share her love, which is really all she ever wanted to do anyway.

With the latest Sugarland tune thumping in my iPod I've changed my mind set completely, effective right this moment, I ain't settlin'.

For weeks everyone has been talking all this nonsense about "New Years Resolutions." Who needs a resolution anyway? I mean, really. I could make a resolution to drink less, see family more...blah blah. But what I really need....what I really need is a big fat write off. Isn't that what businesses do at the end of the year, balance the books, take some write offs? So forget it, forget celebrating day one of a new year, and let's celebrate the last day of an old year. Here's to "write offs."

I'm going to Write Off that I didn't take enough 'me' time last year and now have to go talk to Sarita about it.

I'm going to Write Off that I guilt tripped my parents into staying another day over 4th of July because I love them instead of letting them go home to Max.

I'm going to Write Off that I finished two books that changed my life, but never did finish the third one "Dedication."

I'm going to Write Off that I polished off a magnum of wine with Megan and had a great time doing it.

I'm going to write off that I set out to live the American Dream and failed miserably at it this year.

There are no resolutions on my mind, only one positive thought, those who love me and add value to my life. I've come 90% and fallen short regardless for far too long. Telling my heart what my head says and dangit if I don't listen to it this time - I'm going to walk one-hundred percent for me, and fifty percent for you. Maybe together we'll be a heck of a team.

DISSOLVED

I stepped off the plane in San Diego and went directly to one of my best friend's houses. We had polished off a bottle of wine and discussed my course of action, naturally I stayed over the night. The next morning I called my husband and asked him to meet me at a bench in Shelter Island, the harbor in San Diego. My friend dropped me off at the park bench and left.

I sat nervously staring at the harbor, and the pathway along the water, it was one we'd walked many times with Rio. I thought about what my life in San Diego meant to me, and I thought about what I was losing. In the last moments before he arrived I changed my mind.

It had been a long time since I'd seen Rio, and I was hoping he would have brought her with him. He did not. He sat down at the bench and I broke the silence.

"How have you been?" I asked.

"Horrible," he replied.

The nervous tension was building and after a few moments of complete awkward introductory conversation I began to recap my recent realizations. But rather than call it all off I asked him for six months of legal separation, six months for him to work out his anger issues without my assistance or interruption. Six months of distance to determine if we could rebuild the basis of the foundation of marriage, six months for him to prove to me that he wouldn't abuse me any more. By the time I finished speaking he told me that there was no grey line, we either stayed together and he worked on it or he wanted a divorce. I knew the former was not a solution; I'd spent enough time on the phone with Sarita, and enough time in my head coming to terms with this.

"We tried staying together, and failed miserably, you told Sarita you weren't coming more than half way. That's fine, but that leaves us six months of separation or nothing." I said.

Point blank as if I'd just been shoved out of an airplane he said, "I want a divorce."

I was falling quickly, I hadn't anticipated this.

"Are you sure? This is what you want? Are you sure you don't want to take a few days and think about this?" I asked in complete shock.

"This isn't how a marriage works; we do it together or not at all. I'm sure I want a divorce."

I sat for a moment swallowing that thought then told him that I had already drafted the separation paperwork but would change it to a dissolution of marriage first thing in the morning.

With that he got up and gave me an empty hug, I felt a tear fall as I watched him get in the car and drive away. I pulled out my iPod and tuned into George Strait, I was looking for a specific song, the only one I could force my fingers to press play on was "Easy Come, Easy Go." I sat there a good twenty minutes staring out at the San Diego Harbor thinking about my course of action, and what my next steps were.

The next day I went down to family court and stood in line for forty-five minutes. By the time I got to the counter the chilly county worker told me I needed two copies and a self addressed stamped envelope. I ran down the street to the copy shop she gave me directions to and ran back as quickly as possible before I changed my mind. I stood in line another thirty minutes and by the time I got back to the counter the temperature of the clerk had dropped below zero. She flipped through the documents, double checking the accuracy and I watched page after page containing personal information such as my wedding date, financial detail summaries, and community property get marked like a scarlet letter with a big black "DISSOLVED" stamp.

Once she finished slamming the metal flip stamp into every page she looked up at me, handed me a copy and said, "You have two choices, your partner can be served by a deputy at his place of business today or you can have a friend deliver these documents and sign for them."

I wanted to spare my husband the embarrassment, mortification and utter disrespect and dialed a friend. I recall watching our friend's mouth become dry as he flipped through the pages and asked questions about his role in the process. After he came to the last page he looked up from the documents and simply said, "The DISSOLVED stamp is harsh." My name was officially associated with failure.

The San Diego County Clerk unraveled in less than thirty minutes what we'd spent ten years building using nothing more than a black stamp across a flimsy piece of paper, the same way the ocean tide rolls in and washes away hours of sandcastle building in one fell swoop. Not only was it no longer a happy marriage, it was no longer a marriage at all, and I couldn't hide it anymore.

"You're telling me!" I replied and then I watched him walk away with written proof of my failure.

I let the words "Thank you…" trail off as he left.
I had no choice but to begin creating a new life.

ONLINE BLOG JANUARY 2008
BOUNDARIES & ENTITLEMENT

Boundaries and Entitlement, quite possibly the last two issues in the world I thought I'd ever be sitting on a couch in my therapist's office talking about.

"Learned behavior," Sarita explained, "Lack of emotion for what's right and wrong in situations that affect you deeply is the crux of issues you are having."

Let's be clear, no one has ever accused me of being a shrinking violet; anyone who knows me knows I've always made my opinions on the wrongdoings of the world known.

As a matter of fact, just last night I was in a long line, waiting for quite some time, when suddenly the two people in front of me, let four of their friends 'cut.' There was no hesitation, immediately I knew that I would point out all the moral inadequacies to the girls in front of me, the words flowed from my mouth quite easily without thought. They came from somewhere deep in the gut, something that allows you to quickly and swiftly say, "Excuse me, I find it offensive that you just let these four *insert exploitive here* people in, while the rest of us have been patiently waiting."

Certain things we come to expect from strangers, there are no boundaries, which by my definition might equate to expectations and rules we set for ourselves and others. It seems to me that the people who care most about me are able to cross these boundaries because - plainly and simply - I just don't set them very well. Why is it that I have no sense of entitlement to myself when it comes to my emotions and feelings that originate in same place in my gut that words to a complete stranger can spill out from?

It's difficult to express the sinking feeling when you wake up in the morning and think back without much effort and run out of fingers counting how many times in the last week you opened yourself up revealing every organ. Only to be left over-exposed, and realizing you didn't stand up for what you believed in, right then when your body ached feeling what you felt.

Certain adjectives come to mind; criticism, judgment, violation, infringement, desecration, intrusion. None of these clearly outline the self destructive downward spiral that occurs when you realize that the people closest to you stepped over the line. The only person you can really aim the blame at is yourself, for not establishing these boundaries very well.

Somehow I intend to find a way to establish these boundaries and to feel entitled when they are crossed to act out immediately, without fear of retaliation. And furthermore, to learn to appreciate the fact that if expressing your feelings causes someone to leave, then maybe they really shouldn't be in your life anyway.

I guess the best analogy I have is that my life is similar to a six car pile up on the freeway... half of the people are just there to catch a glimpse of the tragedy and the other half are trained professionals who truly want to help. Throw me that yellow caution tape and pull the line taut…because frankly in this messed up state I'm in right now I just can't tell the difference.

THE FATAL CAR ACCIDENT

It was February when I got the call Mom had been in a tragic accident. I absolutely knew that she was the strongest woman I'd ever come upon, but at that fatal hour, I prayed that she had super human strength. I don't know if anyone can anticipate what it's like to get the call.

"Kayla, it's Dad, I need you to hear me out, Mom's been in a terrible accident, there is one fatality and she's being life-flight to the hospital, your brother is already there, that's all I know right now."

My mind began racing, would she still be there when I got there? If she was there, would she know me? Could I tell her I love her and would she know what that meant? Did she know how much I loved and appreciated all she was to me, in my life? What did I say last when I talked to her last night? I think it was something stupid.

At that juncture in my life I quite literally would not have been able to deal with the loss of Mom. I had made the nine hour drive home more times than I could count, but that time felt like I was trapped six feet under with nothing but a garden shovel to dig myself out.

The accident scene for my mother was nothing short of a miracle, she barely limped away, and the other person did not. The car rolled into a ravine, and she came out with a concussion, broken foot and a fractured spine. She was strong enough to pull her own body out of the car, operating on nothing short of adrenaline.

In the car behind her was a man and his two kids, who avoided the collision. I'd like to think mom was in the accident to save that family. There are things in her mind, she says she can't forget, there are things in my mind I equally can not forget and never will. There are permanent marks in my memory.

It's as if life is a tattoo and each of the incidents is one more prick toward it's completion. Perhaps each person only gets one tattoo; maybe some of us get a few, but the only way to complete your tattoo is by all the life experiences, one prick at a time. At the rate I was moving my tattoo was going to become a full sleeve.

ONLINE BLOG FEBRUARY 2008
EXPECTATIONS

If there's one thing I'm learning, that's guaranteed in life, it's that you never know what to expect, and furthermore - you're likely to be pleasantly surprised or let down anyway...

Because, when you least expect to smile, someone sends you a text that has your stomach aching. When you least expect to cry, you find the tears rolling without explanation.

When you least expect the dog to pee on the floor, she does.

When you least expect a real estate agent to walk in on what was a quite enjoyable Saturday morning shower, it happens.

When you least expect to hurt, you sting like hell.

When you expect to laugh, sometimes you just don't
  think it's that funny.
When you least expect someone to show up at your door
  for a hug, they do.
When you least expect to feel sixteen again, it happens
  - a chaperone to dinner, with a kiss on the cheek
  goodnight...
When you least expect life to happen, it does.

Last Sunday I woke up, dream interrupted by a real estate agent who wanted to show the house. I had thirty minutes to get ready and get out of the house, I had nowhere to go. I showered quickly, and threw on my new jeans, my heels too. Even though I looked cute, I had no expectations for anything exciting to happen. I grabbed Rio, jumped in the car cranked up John Cougar Mellencamp's "Cherry Bomb" and drove with all the windows down and the sunroof open.

I've always been a fan of getting lost; I firmly believe it's the only way to find new roads. And so with no one to report to, and no where to go I took the back roads up and down and through Point Loma...and after the song was about to be over, for the third time, I pulled into a rustic artisan bread bakery in Shelter Island, tied Rio up outside, walked in and picked out a delectable looking cioccolata roll and a café latte.

I sat outside with Rio on the patio and sipped that deliciously hot drink answering questions about my skinny dog and for one minute I was anywhere but there...enjoying life... when I least expected it.

I stand at this intersection "Michaela's Future" all walk signs are green...with one greater lesson learned. Up until last night I thought I just wanted to get where I was going without everything in between. Now I've changed my mind.

I'll get there with all the stuff in between, and a lot stronger, but without expectations of what's to come, or where I'll go, or what I'll become.

Now's the part where I wish mom and dad would take each one of my hands as I step out into the street. Being a big girl sucks.

CONSEQUENCES

There were days I hated living with the consequences of my decision, but I never once regretted it. I started seeing Sarita a few times a week, and I'm sure her emotional documentation chart would have been a dead ringer for the architectural design of a new rollercoaster at Magic Mountain.

Slowly but surely I began to endure every emotion she said I would, from doubt and sadness, to anger and relief; and I lived out the stereotypical events. When I least expected to laugh I laughed so hard I cried, and when I least expected to hurt, I collapsed to the bottom of the shower in a fit of tears and rage.

Eventually I stopped having panic attacks at two-thirty in the afternoon the usual time my ex-husband would come home from work, which was the biggest indicator that I'd done something right. But, three months in, I still had my moments where I completely broke down in hysterics. I watched friends turn their backs and judge me for my course of action. And there were people who disappeared to let me heal. Likewise there were saviors who came out of the wood work as true miracles in life, to help me up when I'd fallen, "The Rebound" was no exception.

THE REBOUND

So I decided to have "The Rebound" sign a friend contract.
I know he was "The Rebound" because by definition, he's
the first person following the ex, who came in and saved the
day, a knight in shining armor who wanted to be more than
friends and simply put, I just wasn't ready. To further compli-
cate matters he was there the night things took a turn for the
worst with my husband, he witnessed the whole thing. He felt
like he needed to rescue my heart, and he didn't understand
why I wouldn't let him near it. He would say everyone else in
my life has the full code to the padlock surrounding my soul
and he couldn't even get a digit. The walls were to protect
me because in the end I knew the relationship would destroy
us both and I'd lose my friend, and the end was inevitable.

I knew the path of destruction we are on, and deep down
I know where our relationship is headed. I tried keeping
him at an arm's distance, but inch by inch, he got closer and
closer. He would treat me better than any man ever treated
me and he loved me with more of his heart than I knew was
possible. And since I didn't know how to handle him, or his
undying love I decided to have him sign a friend contract. I
clearly outlined the rules of engagement.

In order to be friends moving forward we must set boundaries and guidelines, otherwise I fear because I am not ready for a relationship, I will in fact hurt you beyond repair and we will no longer salvage any friendship whatsoever. The rules are as follows:

I can date whoever I want and you can't get jealous

Booty calls are out of the question

You can't show up to my house unannounced

You can no longer dive bomb any man I start a dialogue with at the bar

If you break any of these rules then we can no longer be friends

Initials_____ Rebound _____ Michaela

He signed it, but quite frankly he was terrible at following the rules and I was terrible at punishment. The struggle created horrible tension. He wanted me whole heartedly as his lady and I wanted a friend. My friends would say I was vulnerable and that what he was doing wasn't right. They'd use adjectives like toxic, unhealthy, damaging and hurtful to describe our relationship, but sometimes when you are standing in the eye of the storm; it's tough to see the hurricane.

I attempted to put walls up with him, because I knew something about it didn't feel right, but at the same time, I didn't know what I'd do without him. The ex-husband was still my roommate and sometimes I just needed a place to get away. His house key was like a chunk of gold and lying on his chest felt like buckling my seatbelt, a false sense of security. I didn't know what I would do without him though my gut would tell me I should not put him or any man in the way of my broken heart. So day in and day out I reminded him of the friendship contract, it was the only way I could be clear about my feelings. At the end of the day, I knew I'd be crushed if I lost his friendship.

THE MAN OF MY DREAMS

Enter stage left, Wesley of the <u>Princess Bride</u>: the cliché definition "man of my dreams." It was one of those nights where I shouldn't have even been out, I shouldn't have even given him my number, and I certainly shouldn't have agreed to a first date. After all, I knew how well the whole rebound thing was working out. Clearly I was not very good at setting boundaries or expressing realistic expectations that Sarita and I had talked about.

When we first met I blew him off. I did the stereotypical shove-away Sarita was always warning me about and made no qualms about the fact that I was dealing with a lot emotionally. But from the moment we first spoke I could not deny the way he reached into my heart and made it tingle again, how his wit kept me laughing until my stomach was sore, how his savvy mind made my head spin in the good way that keeps you coming back for more. And how his kiss was like nothing I'd ever experienced. His smile, his confidence, and his touch warmed me at the core.

A few weeks after we began dating I left town for a business trip to Vancouver, I had a brief layover in Seattle. I'd mentioned the travel to him in passing and shared that I was nervous about the big meeting. When my plane touched down in Seattle I turned on my phone to get caught up on work before I got on my puddle-hopper to Canada. The phone buzzed to life and immediately sent a beep indicating there was a text message, it read:

> *I had business in Seattle, my flight landed at the same time as your connection, just thought I'd escort you to your flight to Vancouver*

I had just stepped off the jet way and into the openness of the SeaTac terminal when the second text came through:

> *You look lost* J

And then he appeared behind me helped me with my carryon, grabbed my hand and guided me through the bustle of the airport to my next flight. He was soothing, charming, wonderful and lovely in every way. As our relationship grew, I couldn't help but think he was the perfect partner, sans the timing. I didn't have to pull out the list Dad had me write to confirm it; I fell head over heels for him. My heart was busy focusing on embracing his mind-boggling qualities but my mind was screaming the timing wasn't right.

Sarita immediately recognized it in my eyes when I spoke about him during our sessions, and she knew that whatever he'd done to me was something that had affected me so deeply that it was likely he'd be the only person to pull me up from the depths my heart had sunk to after my futile attempt at marriage. The argument between my head and my heart made me feel like I'd been run through with a sword; I felt the desire to keel over.

She recognized his "push and pull" as a moral struggle in his head and encouraged me to hang on, despite wanting to walk away, no, run. She never questioned the smile that would appear when I would mention his name and she never doubted that he was a wonderful, amazing man with bad timing.

ONLINE BLOG MAY 2008
WHO DOESN'T BRING WINE?

I landed myself some tasty won ton soup and a fortune cookie the other day, I opened it up to reveal this fortune:

Your love life will be happy and harmonious.

I think the fortune cookie companies need to spend a little less time in the production of the cookie and a little more time in Research and Development on fortunes that contain an element of reality.

It's really misleading, I know this because I have a stash of little fortunes in my wallet and not a single one has yet to come true. Maybe they should just add the timeframe in which said fortune will happen. That would be better. Imagine my excitement to see:

Your love life will be happy and harmonious beginning next Thursday.

Then at least it would become a self-fulfilling prophecy, like, "Whoa - it's Thursday my fortune said I'm going get laid!" And by sharing this tidbit with everyone at the bar, it would be more likely to actually occur.

It all began two weeks ago, just before the "man of my dreams" left for Bogota. I planned to cook him a nice dinner at my place. In hind sight we should have ordered take out Chinese, because no sooner than fifteen minutes late, he walks through the front door empty handed. Strike one. He didn't even bring a bottle of wine to dinner. That should have been all I needed as a red flag. But obviously, the blatant red flags that half the population sees are lost on me.

So two weeks later he asks me to join him for dinner at five PM on a Saturday night, which immediately sent up warning signals. But, it happens to be a fabulous sushi restaurant, with a romantic ocean view and he sounded sincere and excited to see me following his worldly travels.

As he pulls out my chair I notice he takes the seat with the ocean view. Strike two. As he starts to wrap up the conversation I suddenly realize that despite I had hoped he and I were picking up right where he left off before his vacation and that he just wanted to spend extra time with me, in fact, the early dinner was because I was Plan B. Now, don't get me wrong, I tried to look at the scenario from all possible vantage points, but no matter how you flipped it, it was just plain disappointing, in every sense of the word.

I quickly split the bill with him and bee-lined for my car, I was being ditched at seven PM on a Saturday night. I kissed him goodnight, one last one for good measure, and told myself that was Strike three. I was utterly and completely disappointed.

It wouldn't have been so bad if my ex-husband hadn't shown up the next day to deliver a dozen red roses and a bottle of Silver Oak. The "man of my dreams" was invited over for dinner and didn't even bring a bottle of Two Buck Chuck (my second favorite following that '03 Alexander Valley Cab).

I will add that after thorough 'bring a bottle of wine' polling: sixty percent fired, forty percent one time hall pass/forgivable offense.

But despite this I'm quickly learning either A. I'm a complete idiot who has absolutely no ability to take the advice of my friends and family, or B. I'm a hopeless optimist who truly believes that everyone means well and will make it right. Regardless of which, it leads to an outcome of frequent circumstances of disappointment.

Now, it's well past my bedtime and I'm a tad delirious, but I need to take a quick moment to point out that the word "blog" is apparently not in the Microsoft Word spell check. Seriously? Can we talk about this? Didn't Microsoft create the concept of a "blog?"

So now I have to stare at that red squiggly line for the next twenty or so minutes, or take an extra click to "ignore all" for something that really should already be in existence in this software program. There you have it, straight disappointing, if I'm being honest.

But what exactly is disappointment? Technically, every word is definable. I took the liberty to look it up, and it has got to - quite possibly be - the loosest definition of any other word in the English language. Ready for it? Here goes:

Disappointment - Noun: The condition or feeling of being disappointed.

Really?! I'm expecting some serious enlightenment courtesy of Merriam Webster, even the Dictionary writers disappointed me. Maybe my expectations are just set WAY too high.

Obviously, rather than quantify it with a definition, I think we should use some examples.

My friends and I had a great time reminiscing in hindsight over some of these examples:

Someone sending you to Mc Donald's with a special order and then using that opportunity for their pre-planned getaway; leaving you standing with -- ughhh, cold hashbrowns.

Someone telling you in a condescending manner they don't 'do' Myspace because "it's really for the under thirty crowd" insulting your age and intelligence when you know they already have one

Getting your "For Sale" sign tagged with that gawd-awful 80's magenta pink lipstick his ex-girlfriend wears with the words "Goodbye Whore"

Taking extra time to hide your favorite kitchen knife when the ex moves out to ensure it's safety, only to realize the psycho went to it's hiding spot and not only took it, but replaced it with a shitty one. (Zing!)

Learning in graphic detail about the first person your ex slept with since the divorce, during the first dance at your good friend's wedding, causing you to run out bawling and attempting to hail a cab in a sundress while holding your shoes (not even frozen yogurt could stop those tears from flowing).

Getting sent to voicemail when you really needed to talk to someone.

Not having a birthday cake or candles on your birthday.

Being taken for granted by someone you loved for nearly ten years.

Looking back on everything you've built only to realize you have to start over again.

See, the kicker about disappointment is that it rears its ugly head when you least expect it. When you are just going about your day, trying to be a positive addition to society you stumble into something crappy and say, "Wow…that was REALLY disappointing." And it takes a little while to stand up, dust off and keep walking skinned knees and all.

During the process of laying out the examples I formulated a new definition, one that is easy to remember and should apply to nearly any disappointing circumstance or person. It was my goody buddy who helped me draw this conclusion without even realizing it.

Disappointment - Noun: Douchebag.

And with this, I now propose a toast with a glass of wine from that bottle that he never brought to dinner, "To Douchebags, without you this blog would never had been completed."

WESLEY BECOMES "MISTER DISAPPOINTMENT"

As the sixth month following the divorce crept up I began to wonder if there was any hope for me. I was utterly and completely scared and confused. Immediately after I posted the "Who doesn't bring wine" blog online the "man of my dreams" emailed:

> *Given I'm an avid reader of your blog I couldn't help but notice the eerie similarities between the gentlemen you describe in your latest blog and myself ;).*
>
> *Talk to you soon.*

Right then I realized I had sabotaged a good thing. I had done this because first and foremost my ex-husband's tools were still in the garage, secondly I was afraid of rejection and lastly, I wasn't ready to screw up another relationship.

Exit stage left Wesley of the <u>Princess Bride.</u> The "man of my dreams" started to distance himself sensing my instability and I began to feel like I'd failed again. My desire to fix what I had single-handedly screwed up became overwhelming and it wasn't long before I was obsessed with fixing the dilemma between us.

The reality was the divorce papers hadn't even made it to the judge yet, and I was far from being ready to open my heart to him. I had spent a good two years teaching myself how to run from my emotions.

One day I decided to take Sarita's suggestion and open up to him. When I finally did it was exactly like that moment Inigo Montoya says to Dread Pirate Roberts (Wesley in disguise), "Who are you? I must know!" And Wesley responds, "Get used to disappointment." He didn't give me anything to work with, but just enough to keep me on the line.

His antics completely stumped Sarita's incredible intellect. Furthermore, she realized that the struggle between my heart and my mind was a good excuse for me to continue running. Her goal was to teach me how to stop running and allow, and it seemed that he might be the perfect resource for this.

It's not that I didn't want to love at all, because I did love deeply, it's that with him it was like I was reliving that moment when Princess Buttercup looks at Dread Pirate Roberts (Wesley in disguise) and says, "You mock my pain," and he looks her directly in the eyes and says, "Life IS pain, Highness."

The "man of my dreams" was quickly becoming "Mister Disappointment," and that was depressing.

ONLINE BLOG JUNE 2008
MY LIEU DE VIE

One year ago today I was married, about to celebrate my six year wedding anniversary.

One year ago today I adopted the cat, Dash, against the wishes of my husband.

One year ago today we purchased the ocean view dream house in Point Loma that came with a big dream lawn that needed to be mowed.

One year ago today, we made a deal. I am highly allergic to grass, (not just slightly, but the type of allergic that they skin test you to determine) and terrified of the weed whacker.

So the deal ensued: I would use the push mower to mow the lawn and he would use the weed whacker for all the edging.

Since the push mower would not cause grass to fly everywhere the affects of my allergies would be minimized, and since I'm terribly clumsy and do lawn work in my flip-flops, avoiding use of the weed whacker would ensure that I would not have any unnecessary trips to the Emergency Room.

Of course, when you go through a divorce and the ex finally moves out, all bets regarding the maintenance of the lawn are called off. So I decided to get a gardener. As it would turn out my gardener was completely and utterly unreliable and was probably shipped back to the penitentiary on a Paddy Wagon. This left the lawn in a state of disarray. Since I was heading out of town on business "The Rebound" said he would get it taken care of while I was gone, but alas, he did not.

So I come home around eleven PM, exhausted from a week long business trip across the country to find my yard looking remarkably similar to the jungles of Costa Rica. Nearly three-feet tall with weeds, I could hardly maneuver my luggage up the walk because the crab grass had completely grown over it. To give you a visual, this lawn was so bad that even the dog wouldn't crap in it anymore.

It took me a full day to contemplate my options and make a decision on what my next steps would be. After much deliberation, I decided I am no prissy girl, never have been, I would tackle it myself.

Standing there in my white, ridiculously short jean shorts, bright neon green t-shirt and my flip-flops I pulled the weed whacker down from its God-like shrine in the garage. I grabbed the extension chord and plugged it in. Then I stood there for a good three minutes mentally preparing myself. It went something like this:

"Michaela, you are strong, you are bigger than the weed whacker. Thousands of people use them every day; just keep it away from your toes. It will be loud – but you will be louder. It will fling pieces of rash causing grass shards at high speed toward your ankles and calves, but you will embrace the sting – and look forward to your shower."

I had already determined the small area along the driveway would be the best starting point. It was at this moment -only after complete preparation- that I started it up. VRROOOOM, for a second my chest tightened and my gut tensed up, but then I drew courage from deep inside and ran full speed ahead at those weeds while screaming, "I'll show you weeds, I'll show you what happens when you try to take over my life," and I did not stop until they were dead, all of them.

At this moment, grinning ear to ear I decided the push mower would never be able to handle the overgrowth in the front yard, and I would weed-whack the entire thing. Mind you, it's six PM on Saturday and half the neighborhood is enjoying a glass of wine and snacking on cheese and crackers waiting for the sun to set over the Pacific Ocean. Nothing was stopping me.

Not five minutes passed before the neighbors started yelling, "Hey Freddie Krueger, put down the chain saw – I've got a real mower you can use for that lawn."

Have you ever seen what happens when a five-year-old takes his Dad's electric razor to his head? Yep, that's what my lawn looked like. The neighbor had no choice but to come rescue me. For selfish reasons, the same way a mother does not want to take her son out after the hair clipper escapade, the neighbors do not want to live next to someone who weed whacked their entire lawn.

The electric mower was a lot quieter than the weed whacker and I suddenly felt a very different wave of emotion. It was not me against the weeds -rage filled and angry about the direct symbolism to the complete and utter overgrown mess of weeds in my life…it was me, with the mower, collectively and decidedly fixing the problem one blade of grass at a time, with precision and direction.

It took me nearly two hours to finish the lawn that day, but some pretty incredible things happened during that time. The light in the house across the street where the old man had died in the winter came on for the first time (the new renters moved in). In the distant horizon the cross from the Baptist Church began to glow against the setting sun during golden hour. And the direction of the wind shifted from the onshore Santa Ana's delivering some relief to my body which was drenched in sweat. At this moment the breeze cut through the overwhelming smell of grass and delivered a salty smell of the ocean, reminding me of the reason I moved to San Diego.

As I paused to look out at the horizon and the ocean waves I realized something wonderful. The lawn was the shade of jade.

During our entire year of living here we had tried to fight the browning grass struggling against the desert weeds and the heat with numerous trips to Home Depot to no avail…

But something had happened during the last few weeks as the lawn grew deceivingly out of control, and now that it was fully exposed it looked more beautiful than it ever had. We had tried to fix it with anything and everything money could buy, but it wasn't until it struggled on its own left raw to grow naturally, that it became effortlessly beautiful.

Today I am divorced, about to watch my seventh wedding anniversary pass me up as another day of the month rather than a celebration. Today I am eternally grateful for Rio and Dash as they remind me every day what unconditional love is. Today the symbolism is undeniable, as my freshly cut grass has never looked so green, lush, and beautiful as it does now.

SPLITTING THE SHEETS

He signed the lease on his new apartment the first week in July.

Behind his voice I heard the strength of a thousand bulls as he said, "So I'll be there around 10am on Saturday, do you mind if I take the fancy rock salts?"

Cold hard math.

"Of course," I stammered out choking back the waver in my throat, "I'm not much of a cook anyway. Maybe someday I can come see your new place."

After a full minute or two of laughing about my kitchen escapades such as blowing up the microwave, twice, his tone changed.

His volume decreased dramatically and became muffled. "Why didn't I love sweeter?" he whispered, almost as if the question was aimed at the universe rather than at me.

Thud. This moment had been looming like an anvil waiting to drop for months. The beginning of the end, suddenly it was all very permanent. The life we had started to build and the items we had collected over the last decade would literally be laid out on the table and we would spend a few hours dividing what took years to build. "Splitting the sheets" as they call it, which I've come to realize is the most heartless cliché in the English language.

Never one to be short on words, "How so?" was all I could muster as a response.

"Why did I let life get in the way?" he began, "I know what I felt and I know what I did, and everyday I try to stomach all my regrets…but I just want you to know, if I could do it all over again, I would. I'd take all the hurt and the pain and the even same ending, just so I could have a moment with you again to show you that you were everything to me."

That thought was more than I could bear, and as I sat there on the other end of the phone, I was silent. I gently brushed away each tear as they slowly fell, one by one.

"I had the greatest thing in the world," he continued, "and I let it just slip through my fingers. You were pitching against the backstop, tossing the ball and I wasn't there to catch it. I got caught up in the race of life and looked past the most important thing; I've paid the biggest price imaginable, I lost my whole world, my best friend, my partner, my better half."

He gave example after example of moments lost in time that he took love for granted. I thought of those moments as if they were yesterday; in his trembling voice I relived them again. Walks with Rio where he says he should have taken my hand and held it, just because I was beautiful. The times in the early morning where I was goofy, without makeup, cooking breakfast saying something nutty that made him laugh, that he should have paused to kiss me, just to let me know I was his everything.

Being on the receiving end of a phone call that should have been nothing more than a financial calculation was nearly unbearable. Some days I truly believed that I made the right decision, and that I didn't fail him, or myself.

Other days I was faced with the brutal reality that it still did ache. When he would admit his wrongdoings it would take every ounce of strength I have to let him suffer. For the first time in our decade together I couldn't take his pain away for him, I couldn't fix it. There wasn't a thing I could do to make it better and attempting to do so would have only cheated both of us.

The person, who I once called my best friend, was quickly becoming a distant memory. And even though I was no longer in love, I missed the comfort of having someone in my life who knew me better than I knew myself. I missed that when his hand was intertwined in mine it felt like a worn in hoodie and jeans, comfortable. I missed knowing that no matter what life tossed my way, I had a best friend to help me through it. I missed my partner and my buddy.

And while I've learned that the human eye can produce an astonishing number of tears, there's only so much the mind can take in one conversation, and in that moment I said, "Can I call you later?"

He always had the same reply, "Sure, but you won't." And he was right.

But that day he replied with this, "Sure, and if you don't, that's okay."

I'm pretty sure that was the moment in which I could no longer maintain the stable front I'd been upholding and the choking-hiccupping-some-form-of-borderline-hysterical-crying began.

As I quickly hit the mute button on the phone I heard him say, "Michaela, are you still there…listen…I, I shouldn't… man, why do I call when I'm at work…I'm so sorry I ruined your day again…if it makes you feel better, at least you aren't in an office standing up against the wall with your face pressed in the corner so no one can see you cry."

This immediately explained the muffled voice he'd been using and the visual of a 6'3, 200 pound plus athletic man standing in the corner at work like a five year old being punished for tormenting the family cat was enough to get me laughing, and I un-muted the phone.

And in true throwing dagger fashion he said, "Keep that up and I might not have you over for dinner!"

Always one to get the last word in I laughed, "Well maybe I don't want your crappy food anyway!"

I glanced down at my wrist and spotted the cross brace-let I'd bought with Mom a few weeks before and then I did the only thing I could think of. For the first time since the nightmare began- I started to forgive which I'd been denying.

The "splitting the sheets" weekend would come and go and I'd be left with half the sheets, and no fancy rock salts, and inevitably I would look around and try to promise myself that I didn't fail.

TO THE WORLD YOU MAY
BE ONE PERSON

"A friend is someone who understands your past, believes in your future, and accepts you just the way you are." anonymous

My text read:

> *Guys, he just pulled out of the driveway...car loaded...Rio and Dash are confused. The beginning of the end...picking myself up off the floor now...trying to dry the tears. Could use a hug soon.*

It was comparable to the moment when I watched the lady behind the counter at the courthouse take all of two seconds to stamp "Dissolved" across the paperwork and erase ten years of effort. When I got home from court that day I got in the shower because I could cry as much as I wanted and the water just washed away the tears.

It was inevitable that splitting the sheets would be hard, but I never expected I would completely lose it as I watched his car pulling out of the driveway, full of boxes and furniture. Maybe I'd been holding it in, trying to be strong for both of us. All I know is as his car turned down the alley, I turned to run for the shower but I didn't make it that far. I barely hit the close button on the garage door before dropping to my knees in the middle of the kitchen. I tried to muffle my hysterical crying by dropping my head in my hands and curling into the fetal position on the cold tile, but the echo in the empty house was just too loud and the neighbors heard the whole breakdown.

With the dog and the cat unable to offer much more than big confused brown eyes, I tried to be strong but the sobbing wouldn't stop.

Sitting in my half empty house, I did the only thing that made sense. I texted my friends. As I sat there shaking uncontrollably the phone started blowing up with notification after notification and slowly I sat up and used the back of my hand to wipe my face to read the text messages one by one. Each one was different, but each one meant something incredibly special; each one was one less tear I cried.

I attempted to fill my home with the most important thing in my life, my friends, even if it was over the cellular waves in the Universe. One even brightened my day by saying that they'd split the sheets so many times all they had left was a napkin. After I picked myself up off the 9th stair of our staircase that afternoon I dredged over to the computer sent an email to every one of them thanking them for their support:

> *To the world you may be one person, to me you are the world…As my friend you probably already know that:*

> *As your friend, if you need me you can call and I'll be there, always*

*As your friend, you know if you want to laugh, or
you want to cry, I'll do it with you*

*As your friend, you know that while I talk way too
much, I can be all ears when you need it*

*As your friend, you know that my calendar is
always loaded, but it's never too full for you*

*As your friend, I probably drive you crazy because
I call, email or text just because something made
me think of you.*

Then I picked up the phone and made two phone calls,
because there were only two people that I was willing to let
hear me like that, my mom and my best friend, Tennessee. I
wasn't sure if Tennessee knew that after all we'd been through
together I really considered her exactly that, my best friend.

"Hi," I began sobbing.

"Oh MJ, today was the day he came to get the stuff?"
she asked.

"Yep, there's nothing left, there's only half. It was so horrible, he got the blue towels, I got the burgundy," I coughed out.

"The towels aren't important. Not at all. This was a big
step toward your new life; we'll go buy you some new towels!
Those leopard print ones you wanted from West Elm," she
laughed back. "You should come downtown with us tonight,
get out of the house, and clear your head."

"Ugh, I dunno…I'll think about it…I would like new
towels soon though, and…Tennessee," I started.

"Yea?" she replied.

"Thank you for being there…always…"

"That's what best friends are for. I love you, MJ."

I realized that symbolism of friendship is the small things you offer. A few days later I stood panting on the side of the road waiting to catch a glimpse of a buddy of mine during the final stretch of his marathon, my frantic waving and hollering caused him to spot me, and we made eye contact and he smiled and waved. Seeing him get a little hitch in his giddy up at mile 24.5 of 26.2 miles made the twenty minute struggle to find parking, the brief shower and the rushed morning all worth it. That's what friendships are all about; taking an extra few minutes of your day to make someone else feel special, and going on blind faith that the moment in which you need them, they'll be there simply because they want to.

Day after day I somehow put on a smiley face and proved to myself with the help of my friends that I was stronger than the moment or the day. Slowly I started to revert back to my usual chatty self, sharing stories and jokes with new people I'd meet and old friends alike.

"The Rebound" continually complained that I rarely mentioned of all the great things he did for me, I laughed when I found this email from him

Things I will still do for you as friends:

Get you a straw

Get you a drink from the bar so you won't have to

Make you the most incredible mixed cocktails

Make you guac on request

*Not let a bartender tell you to put your head up
when you put it down to laugh*

Protect you

Be your Sherpa

Love you with all my heart

So I texted him:

I'm a big girl who is standing on her own two feet.

His immediate reply was:

*You've always stood on your own two feet, now you
just aren't holding anyone else up.*

I didn't have to look far to find a friend who understood
my past, believed in my future and accepted me just the way
I was. Then the bubble burst as the final text came through:

*Speaking of standing on your own two feet, I think
we should probably talk about us soon.*

The problem was there still was no "us," all I wanted was
a lifelong friendship.

ONLINE BLOG EARLY JULY 2008
FAREWELL ODE TO ZEN COUCH

It's charcoal colored, about six feet long and three feet wide and when you sit in it you are only resting fifteen inches above the ground. When I bought it I went into West Elm alone. I'd saved my pennies for a good three months to purchase the newest spring addition "tillary modular seating." The guys at the shipping dock had a bet going with each other that it'd never fit and I'd have to put it on layaway until I could borrow a truck. What they didn't know is that there was no way in hell I was leaving without it. Visions of the Griswold family Christmas tree strapped to the top of a station wagon were coming to mind.

Thirty minutes later, dripping with sweat I closed the back of the ML500, brushed my palms together and grinned like a five year old on the shitter. I heard the guy at the shipping dock say, "Fuck, lunch at Taco Fiesta it is then, who knew she'd be so damn determined to get that fucking thing in there?"

I literally drove the entire seven miles home with my boobs pressed tight up against the steering wheel and my head at a ninety degree tilt half out the window. Heaven forbid I need to change lanes or put the car in reverse or worse, quickly stop, because it was likely the couch would have killed me and anyone in its projectile path.

When I pulled in the driveway I folded up into a reverse pretzel and somehow managed to get the door open and eject myself in a sort of tumble meets cartwheel to the cement. I was the proud owner of my self proclaimed "Zen Couch." The final piece of my superbly designed "Zen Sitting Area" which featured a waterfall, low slung Zen coffee table, and a gorgeous jungle tree whose fronds had a circumference similar in size to the wheel of a fourteen-speed bicycle.

The first challenge was over, and I was staring down the second challenge, getting it inside the house, by myself. This activity was nothing short of completely comical. I managed to get the hand-truck that we'd used time and time again for moving positioned properly at the back of the small SUV. I perched with one foot on the front passenger seat and the other on the driver's seat in a <u>Hidden Tiger, Crouching Dragon</u> pose and grunted like a football player at the line of scrimmage while shoving the ginormous box with all my might.

Eventually, and by eventually I mean a good three hours later, I was pompously resting upon my new private yoga retreat area sipping a dragonfruit flavored *Vitawater* and plugging away at a crossword. I'll never forget the look on my husband's face when he came in.

The first thing he said was, "Where did that come from?" and without waiting for my reply he continued, "How in the HELL did you get that thing in here by yourself?"

I smiled and said, "Determination. Do you love it?"

"Nope."

"You'll get used to it." And thus was the completion of the "Zen Sitting Area."

In retrospect I have come to realize that just fabulous design, and the Zen label, does by no means make a Zen area. Matter of fact, the Zen area has become in every sense of the word the complete opposite of Zen.

Yesterday sealed the deal for the fate of the Zen couch, little did it know I would make a fatal mistake that would cost it its life.

See, yesterday my new roommate moved in and in order to give him some space I left for the latter part of the afternoon. Tennessee and I were dropped off out front around eleven PM, and we headed up the front steps. I stood there for a good minute peeking in the window before spinning to look at her, she was still standing politely behind me when I asked, "So, like, what happens…do I ring the bell or what?"

DINGDONG. I'm waiting, I'm waiting.

When he didn't answer the bell I pulled out the house key and twisted the lock. I shoved open the door and let her in first. I started toward the kitchen but stopped mid-hallway, something caught my attention. What was formerly "the guest bedroom" was now "Sam's bedroom." That's when it hit me.

There was a man living in my house, and with him he brought his stuff. Suddenly my very familiar home was filled with foreign items and my life became very formally different. A new man was now calling my house his home and there was no going back.

I could hear the dryer in the background that I didn't turn on, I could see his computer monitor perched on the desk in the office and his trash can was in my kitchen. Nothing looked the same and for a moment I felt like I didn't even belong, I was simply standing there looking down on someone else's life.

I braced myself against the wall for support with one hand, dropped my purse to the ground and cupped my mouth with the other hand. I had to spew.

I faintly heard Tennessee ask, "Michaela, are you okay?"

I don't cry in front of people.

"Not okay," I managed to reply while shaking my head from side to side.

Me and the Zen couch go way back, see I just hold in those tears until I'm alone, then I plop down sitting cross legged trying to enforce yoga upon stress that is ensuing at the moment, which rarely ever works, so inevitably I am forced to turn to Option B. Option B is when myself and my laptop arrange a face to face appointment with the Zen Sitting Area the next morning and hammer out a journal. It's incredibly healthy, honestly. Who knew it would become more like the couch in Sarita's office than a spa retreat?

"Here, you don't look good, sit down."

That was it. That was the fatal mistake. Because the next words out of my mouth in between my sobs were, "I hate this couch."

I started to tell her story after story, moments on the Zen couch, none of which had a happy ending...

That night that I was dropped on the ceramic tile and got the black eye, remember? I was laying here on this couch while they held ice on my fractured eyebrow.

The night I told my husband that I couldn't do it anymore... I was sitting right here.

The night he came home from counseling and had flowers in his hands for the first time in ten years and I looked at him and realized he just didn't get it, he wasn't going to change, I was sitting right there.

The morning after my ex moved out, "The Rebound" came over with a breakfast burrito because he knew I was so hung over that I might still have been drunk. We ended up spending three hours sitting in this exact couch trolling through every document I have trying to find my birth certificate and the pink slip to my car.

That Saturday night that I got ditched after the sushi date with "Mister Disappointment"...remember I got that text from him four hours later asking if I was still up in North county? "The Rebound" came over, and held me right here on this couch, trying to make it better.

And to top it all off, some of my best nights of sleep have been alone on this couch.

With each story my Pisces friend's eyes got bigger and bigger and by the end she had this fire in her eyes like nothing I've ever seen. "THAT IS IT! You have sat and cried for the LAST TIME on this couch! You know what we're going to do? WE'RE GOING TO BURN IT!" She declared.

"What?!" I replied with a look of utter astonishment.

And then she stood up and yelled with the conviction of a Southern Baptist Minister on a Sunday morning, "YEP! THAT'S RIGHT! You better buck up and get writing your farewell to this couch because we're burning it this weekend! That's exactly what we're doing! We're tagging it with your farewell words in bright red paint we're borrowing G's truck and WE'RE GETTING RID OF THE BAD VUJU ONCE AND FOR ALL!"

Okay. That's just hilarious. The visual of Tennessee and I backing up a Toyota Tundra at the beach on a Saturday night in the company of a couch strewn with hate words in red paint and dancing around a massive Zen explosion like a bunch of tribal Indians at the spit made me laugh out loud. No, not just laugh, roll.

A farewell "Ode to Zen Couch" and you can bet I'll have a real nice time hammering out that little pearl on my laptop this week.

This morning when I went downstairs to let the dog out to pee I glanced over at the Zen Sitting Area and was shocked to see that the waterfall was all dried up. It'd been that long since I had turned it on, it had been that long since the Zen Sitting Area was a serene place for me to relax.

Thus marks the end of the "Zen Sitting Area," and much like the dried up waterfall, my last tears have fallen. I glanced towards Sam's shut door and realized Tennessee was right, this wasn't a man living in my house messing up my Feng Shui, this was a friend who was here to help me on my journey, a friend to help me make new happy memories.

ONLINE BLOG MID JULY 2008
CONEY ISLAND LEMONADE

I'm not sure how we finally got to the point where we knew we had to go our separate ways, but it started a few weeks ago. "The Rebound" and I were at his house laying down chatting about my upcoming Coney Island themed party and I asked him if I could get some of the lemons off his tree for the spiked lemonade. Then somewhere, out of nowhere I blurted out, "I can't go on like this. We'll never work, not until you get a girlfriend."

I recollect that after the words came out I bit my tongue so hard it bled, it was what I was thinking but never had the courage to say. How could I say that to him? How could I look someone in the eye who cared so deeply for me and say something so hurtful?

He let his head fall back and put his hands up to his face. He rubbed his eyes and stayed silent for a good two minutes. And then he said something that shocked me, "You're right, Michaela. I've fought you on this for months now. I'm done fighting. If this is what you want... You got it."

THUD. I'm such an idiot. Of course this is not what I want. Hell no. I want my best friend in my life forever. I want him there all the time telling me everything is going to be alright. But is this fair?

I sat there thinking, crap, what do I do now? Here I am having a great evening with someone that I don't even have to speak to and he gets it, and then I go and open my big blunt Sagittarius mouth because my guilty conscience is killing me and he responds with, "fine, have what you want, leave."

I was so pissed at myself I could hardly see straight and I felt fury building up inside my chest. I hated myself for what I was doing to "The Rebound" and I hated that for the first time in months he was able to let me go. I got up and headed over to his sliding door and paused to peek out the window at the lemon tree overflowing with lemons in the far corner of the yard. Then I grabbed Rio's leash and turned to look at him...

"Say goodbye to your Stepdaddy Rio."

And then I left. Four days we didn't talk. No text, no emails, no anything. I knew this day would come, but after six months of constant 24/7 contact I had no idea how excruciating it would be.

On the fifth day he called. His clarity was astonishing as he began drilling questions and statements at me like a military sergeant, at some point he blurted out in anger, "Michaela, I can't see you ever again."

The thought of never seeing the man who helped me through the toughest times and had provided a comfortable place for me to sleep when my own home and bed was the last place on earth I wanted to be was more than I could bear. Right then, I became too weak to finish the dialogue we began. I told him the rest of the conversation would have to wait, that I'd call him the next day. He told me that this was classic and to quit running. But I hung up. He'd been dealing with it this long; one more day wouldn't kill him.

Then I called Tennessee, I told her that I knew this was a long time coming but that I held his heart in my hands and I didn't want to let it go. I couldn't. I told her I was mad at him for loving me too much. How could he let himself get so close that now we couldn't even have a friendship? I spent months begging him not to love me, promising him that I couldn't give back.

"Michaela, if you truly love him you have to let him go," she said.

And she was right.

I called him the next afternoon as I promised I would. As we sat on the phone both crying, he asked, "If you could have anything you want right now, what would it be?"

"Selfishly, if I could have anything I wanted it would be one more beach walk with you and Rio at six PM barefoot, one more hug at nine-fifty PM while the fireworks are going off at Seaworld after walking Mission Bay, one more tipsy Sunday afternoon after a Mai Tai and Ahi Poke. It would be one more night of you telling me everything is going to be okay. It would be you coming here right now with FroYo to brush away my tears and tell me that I look the most beautiful you've ever seen with puffy swollen eyes."

"Please stop," he said.

"But for the first time ever this isn't about what I want. What I really need, right now more than anything, is to never see you again." I coughed it out.

And in true fashion, always thinking of me before himself he asked, "But, how will I get you the lemons?"

I hadn't anticipated that, but I had a plan, "I'm going for a run with Rio, I'll be gone forty-five minutes." I said.

I can't remember the last time I ran so hard, pushing up the steep hills of Point Loma. I was short on air as memory after memory; snapshot after snapshot of him saving the day, rescuing my broken heart came to mind. As I crested over the top of the street on my return, I swear I saw his truck, and I ran faster toward it, but he was gone.

As I walked up the front steps arms extended high above my head panting I saw the largest bag of lemons I'd ever seen in my life and I clutched my chest to stop the sting. He'd also left the most beautiful shag rug ever made to go perfectly with my new bougy couch that replaced the Zen. I unleashed Rio and sat down on the front steps to catch my breath. And I texted him:

I'm dying, It's me, It's you, It's perfect. Love You.

The day of the Coney Island party I started to get to work on the lemons, I was making a complete mess of the juice and the rinds and I had two people helping me because it was far too much for one person. As people arrived they started happily drinking the delicious concoction, and I couldn't help but chuckle that even though he didn't come to the party, he still managed to be there. So typical!

Sometime around seven PM, I felt something in my gut and I glanced up just in time to hear someone at the party say his name. It had felt like forever since I'd seen him and it'd been well over a week since I'd spoken to him. My heart skipped watching him open the gate.

I tripped over the beer pong table and fought my way through the crowd in the yard and stopped dead in front of him as he wrapped his 6'4 frame around me. There were quite a few people at the party who were stunned and many whispering back and forth but it didn't matter, all I heard was what he said as he pressed his head firmly against my ear, "I'm so sorry I'm weak, I just needed one more hug."

Standing on my tippy toes I hugged him back as tight as I could. I told him the lemonade turned out great and that it was a huge success. I'm pretty sure he didn't hear a word of it though, because the next thing he said as he took my face in his hands was, "You smell like citrus and you look like a slice of heaven."

And then he left.

IT'S JUST ME, HERE I AM

The roommate had lasted all of two weeks before he announced he couldn't pay the rent, which was fine because we'd finally gotten an offer on the house. I found myself in the downstairs office shuffling through papers trying to find a document that needed to be faxed to the real estate agent. The office was a room I had avoided since the beginning of the divorce. It just conjured up bad memories.

That's when I spotted the little piece of paper tucked in the manila folder of real estate documents. It was labeled "Game Plan."

> *Update my "who I'd like to meet" section of social networking site to "myself in six months"*
>
> *Create a bucket list (things I want to do before life is done) and tackle at least one of them (can I really try ALL the FroYo in San Diego County?),*
>
> *Sign up for Krav Maga (self defense to ensure I have the strength to never, ever let anyone hurt me ever again),*

Find my true friends (and remove the unhealthy ones from my life),

Redecorate/Repaint (interior design is one of my favorite things),

Get back into my hobbies (golf, singing, photography, horseback riding, book club, acting classes and so much more),

Find my style again (clothes, furniture, anything I can associate a Michaelaism with),

Use Michaelaisms (to the annoying point in which everyone is using them, Shift-Delete, Borderline Amazing, Um-can we talk about this?, Choataly, For Sure Sure), Ridi-ka-lus

Learn it's okay to cry (and let others witness that happen),

Love (and forgive with all my heart),

Find laughter (and share it with anyone who will listen),

Find the inspiration to do what my heart knows I'm on the earth to do, something for the greater good

I realized that a little over six months ago when I had created the game plan I had been wearing black knee length gym shorts, an oversized white T-shirt I'd proudly obtained from the Rock N Roll Marathon I had run, Asics running shoes and silver hoops in my ears which added balance to the outfit.

It wasn't that I didn't like who I'd become, no, not at all; rather, I didn't like who I'd let go. Sometime during the course of my marriage I'd become a skeleton of who I used to be. I had abandoned all the color in my life to become a shade of grey, simply to avoid conflict and make room for all the emotional hiding that I was doing.

Underneath all those layers of skin I'd built up to protect myself was a girl who had been taught from a young age to get up and dust it off, a girl who had pizzazz and knew how to laugh in the toughest of times. The process of finding where I'd left her was going to be a painful one.

An enabler was the term used to describe my behavior. I was so good at covering up what was really going on in my marriage and protecting my husband from his own issues that some said I was even to blame for him not getting help sooner.

In the process of elevating him up on that pedestal my clothes went from Nordstrom to Old Navy, the colors I painted in the house went from yellows, teals and reds to ice, tan and pale green. I had become a boring display at Levitz instead of the vibrant Crate & Barrel I used to be.

But I knew I tackled everything in life with incredible gusto and the journey to find Miss Michaela instead of Mrs. Ex Husband's wife was no small feat, hence the game plan.

Staring at that hand written piece of paper six months later I realized that the first few bullets were much easier to achieve than the final two, laughter and inspiration.

Laughter

When I least expected it, I met "Mister Disappointment" who had the ability to make me smile on my toughest days and laugh out loud when I didn't think I could. In the beginning, I firmly believed he was nothing more than a distraction, a mere vacation resort for all that my mind was going through. It was only after he was gone that I could admit he was fireworks in all the right places for no clear reason. He appeared in my life when I least needed it and left when I least expected it. Our relationship was incredibly short lived and left me out of place and confused.

To help me grasp our relationship and consequent lack thereof I frequently brought him up to Sarita. "I just don't understand his push-pull, he's in, he's out, he's here, he's not. It's like he doesn't want me, but he can't let me go. I just want to move on."

"Your eyes dart when I say his name aloud and I see through your smile that your eyes carry pain."

I quickly find extreme interest in the pattern on the rug and opt to stay silent, so she continues, "Please explain that to me."

She knows the answer before I speak. "The future," I begin.

"I wish I could take that pain away," she offers.

After an uncomfortably long silence consisting of staring at my legs double crisscrossed and extended hovering over the elegant carpet I take a deep breath and a long sigh I look her straight in the eyes and say, "It's because he was the definition of the future."

Looking back I realized he was required to be in my life, to help me find me. "Mister Disappointment" was a snapshot of what happiness could be, his ability to bring out the witty side of me was effortless and I still chuckle thinking about some of our countless text messages and silly moments together. With the pain I endured through my relationship with him, I enjoyed gut-twisting laughter.

Inspiration

Clearing my head and my heart of "Mister Disappointment" was not easy, but to quote an old saying, "When God closes a door he opens a window." The moment which I let the hope of "Mister Disappointment" go was the moment I was able to clearly see the direction I should be headed.

Like a lily in the spring my heart opened back up and I was fortunate enough to meet new people who helped me find my inspiration, one is an amazing writer who endured the loss of his wife to a battle with cancer, his words and writing touched me very deeply. The second was a singer/songwriter whose talents and drive to accomplish his dreams made me pause and smile.

Each day I thanked God for my family who was there on the days when no one else was. The days where I was wandering aimlessly down a dark alley.

The biggest part of overcoming what I'd been through, the one thing I couldn't list in the game plan, was learning to trust again.

I needed to learn to trust myself and to trust others, to open up my heart and look someone in the eye and say, "Here, have a little piece of this."

As the fax machine hummed the beep of indicating sent delivery confirmation I realized that you wouldn't recognize the girl who wrote that game plan six months ago as one in the same. I walked from the office into the downstairs bathroom and stood in the mirror.

I was wearing a button down brown tank top with white butterflies on it, a lacy neon green bra just barely peeking out the top, blue corduroy slacks that rested loosely on my hips, and French-tipped manicured toes peeked out the top of a brand new pair of flip-flops. A faded burgundy visor poorly held in a tousled mess of blonde hair and was poised on top of my head like Pebbles and BamBam from the Flintstones. The outfit was complete with a set of ridiculously childish dangly orange sea turtle earrings I had bought well over seven years before. Best part was, I didn't give a pootananny if anyone doesn't like it *insert emoticon with the little tongue sticking out here*.

I had learned to let go of the piece of me that used to be so concerned about what others would make of my life, or my mess (whichever you choose to refer to it as). I walked proud carrying all my baggage tucked nicely in my Northface backpack, far enough from my soul to let me move on, but close enough to my heart that I'd never lose the lessons learned.

Furthermore, as I began to tell new stories, I told them with so much emotion that people passing by would stop to catch a glimpse of the ruckus. I usually ended up finding myself so funny that I'd be crying before getting to the punch line. My ring finger showed no tan lines, no sign of my past and around my neck was a small sterling silver cross which the sun danced upon to reflect a glorious future. I had no one to answer to, no one but myself. My motto became "It's Just Me, Here I am."

CO-DEPENDENCY & AN ALCOHOLIC

It had been a quite a few weeks since the Coney Island party when "The Rebound" showed up unannounced and drunk. This time, I was at a crowded bar when he stumbled in completely annihilated and announced that he'd come all the way across town just to see me. It wasn't the first time, but I was certain it was going to be the last on my watch.

My friends were embarrassed, as was I, and he was completely intoxicated. Yet I gave him the benefit of the doubt and asked him how he'd gotten there. He told me he'd left a bar downtown where his friends had been, he'd driven his truck, it was parked outside. I played nice, sweet and innocent just long enough to take his keys.

I wasn't sure what possessed me; I think it had something to do with all the therapy regarding boundaries and self entitlement. I was tired of seeing him in a drunken stupor, and I was tired of feeling guilty for his behavior and even worse, somehow responsible for anything he might do to himself or anyone else.

I had recently learned that just a few months ago, the driver who caused the collision involving my mom was under the influence of methamphetamines and liquor. He was decapitated in the accident and nearly killed my mom, too. A few years before my brother's best friend died drinking and driving and my brother now has a tattoo on the inside of his arm – the one he shuts the driver door with in memory of his friend.

With "The Rebound's" keys in my hands I stared at him coldly as he playfully attempted to grope me. I was utterly repulsed and I told him so. I told him I was even more disgusted that his friends would let him get in the car like this. That's when he said, "I did it for you. I wanted to see you. I'd do anything for you."

At this moment I grabbed his arm and literally drug him kicking and screaming out to the car. I told him I was not the reason for his alcohol problem, and that he'd been drinking long before me, and would be drinking long after. I told him that would be the last night I'd be his downfall and he needed to get some help. It would be the last night I'd wonder if he made it home safe.

I drove him back to my place to let him stay the night and he passed out within a few minutes. The next morning when I took him back to his car, he told me he hated me as he pulled the parking ticket off his windshield.

A few days later he phoned me simply to get the last word in ending our entire relationship by saying, "You chose this for us, I'll never forgive you, and calling me an alchy won't soon be forgotten."

To hear him repeat back my words in his own slang stung, I didn't mean to hurt him, I just knew his problem was bigger than I could handle.

That day we ended our relationship permanently.

ONLINE BLOG EARLY AUGUST 2008
DETOX AND JUDGMENT

The girls and I decided to board a jet for a girl's trip to Puerto Vallarta. Tennessee and I joked as we were heading to the airport that the "All Inclusive Resort" is the perfect example of gluttony that American tourists thrive on and we fell prey to the concept of taking our denieros to Mexico for a "girl's weekend" consisting of swimming in the ocean, reading, drinking, and the night life.

And after a few days of drinking enough tequila to keep the Mexican tummy nasties away I was ready to switch to water. The hotel claimed it was filtered, and I was thirsty as hell. So literally in the three final hours before we left to head back to the States I consumed two full glasses of water.

The three of us girls were sitting in the shuttle van waiting for our transport to the airport. I was joking that the "All Inclusive Couples Resort" not only added a good four pounds to my previously toned thighs but also helped the divorce healing process immensely! I mean, really, what better way to get over the ex than throwing yourself in the middle of an infinity-edge swimming pool of newly happily-married's so all the women stare at you like you're a shark amongst a pod of dolphins?

Forget the fact it's identical to the resort I got married at seven plus years ago – the only way to face your fear is to dive in both feet first, just one more item for the "list of pain left to swallow" list. They should add that to the Divorce for Dummies book - Girls Trip Singles Vacation at the Couples HoneyMoon resort- CHECK!

I continued to joke that starting with those two glasses of water I was on complete detox.

The celebrity mags say Detox = Rock Bottom, so I knew that was a tad extreme, but comical nonetheless.

Besides, I thought I'd hit rock bottom last year when I was dropped face first on the kitchen tile and spent the night on the floor in the bathroom. I thought the definition of rock bottom was staring in the mirror at empty irises that belonged to a girl I no longer knew combined with a busted eye socket and bleeding grout-destroyed chin.

I was wrong. Rock bottom happened August 4th, 2008 at about eleven PM.

It was a full twenty-four hours after the three of us had touched down safely in San Diego. The house was just about to close escrow and a friend was over helping me pack. I told her I didn't feel well. Matter of fact, I felt incredibly sick. She took the hint and left a bit early. I barely shut the front door behind her when the projectile vomit began. I grabbed my mouth with one hand, cell phone with the other, and sprinted to the bathroom.

I have no idea why I grabbed that cell phone, gut instinct I suppose, but thank God I did! In the course of the next four hours I lost all the ability to physically move my body.

The first hour I spent deciding moment by moment which end to service first in a violent mess of expulsion. It was midnight, it was pitch black, and it wasn't stopping.

I texted four people in one mass text: my ex-husband, Tennessee, "The Rebound" and my brother:

> *If you don't hear from me in the morning, please check the house.*

"The Rebound" naturally left me to die. And as it would turn out, Tennessee was living a similar fate (Montezumas

Revenge to a much lesser degree, she didn't drink the water, she only had the ice) at her house across town. My brother texted:

CALL MOM & ER

And I heard nothing from my ex-husband.

By 1:30am I was curled in fetal position, completely trembling, my throat was destroyed from vomiting over sixteen times, not to mention the pain from what had come out the other end. I couldn't feel my fingers or my toes. I couldn't swallow and I barely had the energy to breathe. I was dying. Alone.

I was literally living out my biggest fear. In my weakened shattered state of confusion I was panicking that literally, there was no one, my family lives nine hours away by car.

So I did the only thing I knew to do, out of habit I dialed my ex-husband, thinking ten years together must stand for something at a time like this.

In a shaky barely legible voice I said, "I can't stop throwing up, I'm very ill, I don't know what to do."

"It sounds like food poisoning Michaela, you'll be fine."

I eeked out, "No Mexico."

He hung up.

Seconds later he texted:

> *Girls trip to Mexico huh? No sympathy here, you made your bed now lie in it.*

That's when I gave in and called Mom. In between gagging, choking and crying Mom begged me to hang up and call 911.

I lay on the cold tile in the bathroom surrounded by my own mucous splatter, reeking of bodily fluids remembering that night in October, and I began to wish for death. I survived about another thirty minutes of wretched pain before realizing if death was what I wanted, I was going to get it, on the cold tile in the same bathroom.

That's when I dialed 911. The paramedics arrived within three minutes and carried me out of the house on a stretcher, my vitals were completely failing and next thing I recall was full sirens to the ER. I have never once in my entire life been a passenger in an ambulance. I was wheeled into an ER packed full of people with head injuries, strokes, and dripping bloody wounds.

I laid there draped in a white gown, on white sheets staring at white walls, surrounded by doctors, nurses and other patients, but I was completely alone. I moved my head just enough to vomit in the bucket they'd given me, I was fading and my vision was blurry. Through my foggy eyes the huge needle providing saline fluid to my dead body became clear as glass and I realized I'd hit rock bottom.

Not sure where my body found the liquid to provide tears, but slowly they dripped one by one, and I didn't even have the energy to wipe them away.

I had made my bed, I better lie in it.

And lay in it I did. For seven hours I laid in that hospital bed replaying my life of late, my choices, and my fears. I looked death right in the face and I told it to piss off.

Thanks to mobile Facebook status updates by 6:30am the next morning I was surrounded by warm texts and emails, phone calls and offers of assistance. I realized that there were a massive number of people I could have texted or called the night before and many of them expressed frustration that I had not.

Somewhere deep-down my soul made the decision to provide more clarity on the decisions in my life than I ever could have imagined. Going through those eleven hours changed my mindset and my path.

I received a pseudo joking text message reply from "Mister Disappointment" after he checked in and I told him:

> *The ER wasn't that bad, I'm a glass half full kinda girl*

He replied with:

> *Leaving glasses empty is what sent you to the ER, sometimes it's okay to leave them half full*

His text poured salt in an open wound. Just weeks before I'd cast that stone, I'd passed that judgment. I was too exhausted to reply in that moment, but when I finally did I gave him everything I had. I literally opened my heart and said, here it is – look at it, touch it, but don't ever pass judgment on it again.

> Me: *back to the living, reread ur text. i'm really upset that i have given u the misconception that i drink a lot, probably hurts the most bcuz i really pride myself on self control, and i know i've failed in every way with you. I'm sorry.*

"Mister Disappointment:" *i see the post drinking mellon collie is kicking in. remember these feelings are only temporary ;)*

Me: *No, in all seriousness this nomenclature with you is my fault and it kills me. It's not enough to tell you I'm here writing, reading, running rio - I know ur heart tells u better - you didn't make a bad judgment call with me. i can't deny u felt right in every unexplainable way. for all sorts of great reasons u've been smart to give me space, the timing had been shitty. and if we can't see each other again short of an accident thatd hurt - but i know i can't dwell on ur judgment of me. i would have loved to have this convo with u in person walking on the beach, but i'm resolved the time wasn't right. I don't bash u-ever. If anything everyone around me knows u were amazing 2 have had my heart like this. don't text me back that i'm crazy - all i ever wanted was for u to know how i felt and still tell me to go. i realize now that it's not ur job. i had to suck it up and do it on my own. ugggh. u got me tho, can't change that - the thot of u still makes me smile.*

ps it's spelled 'melancholy' and the near death experience prompted this text, lucky u.

"Mister Disappointment:" *whoa, just brought my iPhone to its knees, in all seriousness, I never meant to hurt you.*

He who is without sin cast thy first stone.

"EU" CODE WORD FOR A BLASÉ TERM

I'd recovered from the stint at the ER and the house was almost completely packed. I'd spent weeks mentally preparing for the move, it was the last thing the ex and I had between us. I'd opted for a roommate situation rather than getting my own place. There weren't a lot of apartments available in the middle of summer and Tennessee had recently met a guy who had a big house in Mount Soledad and was looking for a roommate. He also came with a dog and a swimming pool. It seemed like a logical idea to have a transition house, because going from a big three bedroom ocean view house to a tiny apartment would have been stark.

In general I was at peace with the way things were unfolding, I had seriously decreased the amount of texting I was doing with "Mister Disappointment." I hadn't spoken to "The Rebound" in weeks. I was finally ready to leave the dream home behind me, and I'd be out on some pretty healthy dates.

I had just met someone that was wonderful, not to mention incredibly attractive. We spent a few hours chatting at a park and his piercing eyes looked right through mine all the way back to the depths of my mind.

He never once asked a question about what kind of music I liked, or what plans I had for the weekend, he didn't much

care. He was a thinker. He saw right past my friendly escapades and started strategically asking me questions that would
pin my soul to the wall. I'd like to say that it was in this
moment, where his mind was calling my heart to the battle
lines that I knew I'd never kiss him. It's not that we didn't
have chemistry; it's that we didn't have *that* kind. I knew he
felt the same way.

When we went back to his place I intentionally found
myself sitting across the room. I didn't think much of it and
I was pretty focused on eating fried chicken while picking
his dog's hair out of my mouth and simultaneously keeping
her wet kisses at bay. I was having no trouble knocking back
my third Alaskan Amber.

Curled up on his couch I sat mutilating the chicken to
get all the crunchy skin off and started to consider my recent
dilemma in between large mouthfuls of juicy white meat. I
figured now was the time to dive in, if we were going to be
friends I might as well.

"I meet these wonderful guys, who are cute and friendly,
sweet, comfortable, funny and entertaining and for some
odd reason, it's like I've got a wall up. It's like I'm just not
interested. I have incredible clarity on it too. It's not like I
sabotage the relationship, but I'm not investing in it either,
I just don't much give a damn." I said.

All of a sudden the sound of him smacking on the chicken
ceases and he cocks his head in a tilt and puts his lips tight
together, which in hindsight I realize was a look of disappointment and said, "Well, it's obvious you're emotionally
unavailable."

Then he went on yammering about how he was too, when
I interrupted, "What'd you say? Emotionally unavailable?"

"Yeah," he tossed a brutal fast pitch at me in his laid back-I'm an artist/thinker- passive way as he was swallowing mouthfuls of fried chicken and cream soda.

I hate that. I hate that the phrase is big and it comes with some pretty large connotations, and I think I hate more that it confirmed he was in fact reading my mind back at the park.

I left that night obsessing over this new phrase. I started running it by anyone and everyone who would listen and what I learned is, half of the world is emotionally unavailable. Right then I began to realize that even "Mister Disappointment" was emotionally unavailable which explained a lot and also made me feel less crazy (even though I was still thoroughly enjoying our fantasy text message relationship).

I pondered the emotionally unavailable concept for days on end. Anyone I would mention "EU" to would go into great detail to explain their personal state of emotional unavailability or stories of someone they know who was emotionally unavailable.

So through great social research study (aka, observing friends in social settings, happy hours, wine bars, nights out, deep conversations and texts) I learned that emotionally unavailable comes in all shapes and sizes, for all different reasons and with all different ways of expression. And, someone can be emotionally available to one person and not to anyone else, or emotionally available to everyone except one person.

I was thinking about how best to gather all of this social studies research in a way that would apply to the masses, make a tad bit of sense and still express what I'm trying to say, which in and of itself was mind boggling. I began to think I could write an entire book on the subject, but then realized someone with more credentials had probably already done that.

It was only two days before the big move. I was sitting on the new bougy couch, staring down my crossword puzzle, knocking back an Alaskan Amber, and eating some potstickers, picking Rio's hair out of my mouth thinking about what a bitch it was for an earthquake to occur the same day I tried to get renter's insurance when the door bell rang.

A guy had arrived to pick up the last of the furniture for sale. I looked over at the dog and she hadn't moved. Not even a millimeter.

That's when it hit me, even the dog was EU.

A few weeks ago, strange random people started coming into the house to pick up furniture they'd bought via my myriad Craigslist ads. At first it was something Rio cherished, it was a good fun time. People showed up and gave her a little attention. It didn't matter how short the amount of time they stayed, it broke up the monotony of her day and took her mind off the fact that she doesn't have the life she used to have.

People continually came to the house and each time they'd go her small world had been slightly changed, leaving one less thing surrounding her that she used to call her own. Eventually the pain of the loss overtook the excitement and she just became overwhelmed and confused. Instead of running to the door bouncing each time the bell ringed greeting a new person with her overly friendly style, she stayed put, remaining tucked away from the action, while observing from a distance.

She had put her walls up and wouldn't let her guard down. Day in and day out, people came in, and they took what they wanted and they walked out.

Then it came to a climactic point, the packing tape on the final moving box was sealed up, slowly every last ounce of familiarity had been packed away. I recognized the glazed over look in her eyes. It was sorrow and it was fear.

But I knew where Rio had been, and I could say with complete confirmation nothing would ever be as bad as the abuse she endured at the race track, and while she enjoyed a comfortable life for awhile, she had coast lines of uncharted territory ahead of her. Without the burden of excess she'd be able to explore every one of those beaches.

But, life was about to drastically change for her, all that was familiar to her, the house, the neighbors, and her nightly walks would all become a memory. The one thing they say is that in time, the bad memories fade and all that's left are the good ones. The people that truly love her don't care where she lives whether it is a house with a huge yard, a tiny room in Mount Soledad or an apartment in North County. They would continue to follow her, if not for anything more than the fact that they believe in her journey.

Emotionally Unavailable was the look in the dog's eyes when I threw the last of her toys into a box and sealed it shut. Life was about to drastically change again.

GIVING GRACE

The next week Mom and Dad came into town and helped me move what remained of my divorce into storage; there was no room for my stuff at the transition house. The room was only available for me to rent through December, just a temporary situation until I found the right apartment. So I selected a handful of things I couldn't live without, the rest went into long term storage.

That day was eerily similar to that fateful day in 1992 when we hitched up the trailer for the move to Georgetown. There were blaring differences, the first being that the majority of my stuff would be waiting for me in storage, when I was ready to retrieve it. The second was I didn't have my family to weather the storm but my new roommate was incredibly kind, understanding and helpful.

And the last was that as I was selecting what few things I would bring, I realized I thought of myself last. The first things that went to the transition house were Rio and Dash's. Above all I was worried about how they would handle the change.

Mom and Dad ended up staying with me at my new roommate's house for the first few nights and having them there made all the hurt easier to stomach. The first night I woke up around two AM bawling. I jumped out of bed and stubbed my toe on everything in the unfamiliar room, eventually I managed to make my way down the long hall toward the guest bedroom where my parents were sleeping soundly.

"Shit Sis, you scared the crap outta us," Dad started.

"Tom, what's going on?" Mom muttered.

I jumped in bed between them and cried. A few days later I cried again when I dropped them off at the airport.

I'd been living with the new roommate for about a week and had finally come to terms with the place I'd put myself in and this juncture in my life.

I thought that the pain was over when I found myself sitting with my soon to be ex-husband outside family court for over two hours waiting to enter the building to go through the metal detectors for the final hearing. The court system calls it "the final judgment." The sale of the real estate expedited the divorce process. I was patiently awaiting the single status technicality and so was he.

Two hours perched on a rock wall surrounded by the other losers in line gives a person plenty of time to reflect on the mistakes that one has made. We had more than enough time to talk but in the first thirty minutes we sat quiet.

I hadn't seen him in weeks, he looked skinny, depressed, scared, and sad and mostly he looked dead to the world. As I glanced him over I wondered how I'd found the strength to let him become this.

After a very long awkward silence he muttered, "I hate that I was a monster."

That's when the tears welled up in my eyes as moments of abuse flashed through my mind. I so badly wanted to apologize aloud for him, but one glance at the people around me indicated that I couldn't defend him anymore.

Furthermore, the only thing he wanted was the one thing I'd always begged him for, mercy.

He wanted me to hear him out, no matter how much it hurt me. So on this final judgment day I did just that. I listened.

He struggled to find the words, and then he finally found them. "You were young and innocent, and I was selfish. I stole your youth…It's like when you have a bad day, and there's a half gallon of ice cream and a spoon, and once you've started you can't stop, no matter how hard you try. And you know it's not right, you know there's nothing good about it, you are repulsed at your inability to control yourself, but you keep doing it anyway…"

Holding my bottom lip tight I stared off the other direction and offered a nod.

"And since you love it so much, it somehow justifies it in your mind that it'll be okay just this one time. But, then every time you are depressed, you go back and do it again…"

I looked down at my feet, hoping if I stared long enough my mind would only see my shoes.

"Unfortunately life doesn't afford you a do-over," he finished.

I wasn't sure what visuals he saw in his head when he told me this, but I knew what I saw, moments that made me wince.

Family court was about to open and for the first time that morning I felt the rock wall digging into the back of my thighs and shifted positions. Much like our first date we were side by side, our legs were dangling over the edge and we were staring at a future; and we were still half the age of everyone in line around us.

Anyone walking down 6th Street that morning would never look at him and see a monster or stare at me and see an abused victim. They would see a handsome man aware of his evils but focused on becoming a better person. They would see a very clear headed beautiful lady full of life and stronger than many. They would see two respectable individuals who are much better off apart than they could ever be together.

Two young bodies, but two old souls who shared friendship and learned more lessons than many live in a lifetime; two kids no longer pretending to be adults, because somewhere along the way, they grew up. Both guilty, both innocent, both wrong and both right.

We were humble. We forgave each other for love and for life and we both had a second chance to be the people we'd always hoped we'd become.

The café down the street lit the neon sign to 'open' and as I got up to get us breakfast I asked him if he could keep an eye on my backpack while he saved our place in line. It was the last thing we would do together.

What he said next reminded me of the reason I married him in the first place…his sharp mind and hilarious wit.

"Sure…Wait! NO! You don't have any weapons of mass destruction in there do you?"

I started laughing hysterically and said, "Wouldn't that be classic, leave your soon to be ex-husband with a backpack full of Jihad paraphernalia before you enter divorce court on the pretense you're bringing him a latte and a McMuffin."

It was almost embarrassing how loud we were laughing as he crackled out, "Yeah, 'cause as soon as my ass'd get out of the slammer, we'd be going to trial, none of this mediator bullshit."

I paused before I headed down the street, looked him in the eyes and said, "Know what? You didn't steal my youth. I had a best friend to laugh with during ten hard years of life. Your do-over starts today, it's just not with me."

In that moment I knew whatever happened to him, for the rest of his life, I'd always hope the best for him. If losing everything was what I had to do, the salvation made it worth it. My friend Carmen called it 'giving grace.'

And if some say history doesn't repeat itself, here I was, twenty-eight years old, living proof, starting my life over, just like my parents had done all those years before.

ONLINE BLOG LATE AUGUST 2008
SAVANNAH'S DAD

Her name is Savannah. She is utterly remarkable and indescribably wonderful in every way and everything she knew she learned from him, an unspoken promise of a past he used to have. And every morning when she rolled over for a belly rub her eyes reflected a glimpse of his heart.

If Sarita had told me that all these lessons on boundaries would be tested in the most extreme way imaginable I would have casually laughed at her, because I seem to have become a poster child for divorce. I quite literally have somehow managed to stumble into every possible divorce scenario. Moving in with Savannah's Dad is no exception.

Savannah's Dad met Tennessee on match.com, neither had a liking for the other, but somewhere amidst their incredibly short dating experience, it was decided for me that I should be his roommate.

I say "decided" because I've come to learn that everything Savannah's Dad does, he does systematically. He is goal oriented to the nth degree, he keeps score and he gets what he wants. He's picky and judgmental, he's downright bossy and he's always right. By the way, you should already know that by now.

Savannah's Dad is thoughtful, sweet and caring. He's sincere and questionable in the same sentence, not because he's manipulative in a devious premeditated sort of way, he might be one of the nicest people I know, but he's driven to the point of success beyond emotion.

Getting in the way of his pen when he's putting it to his mental checklist is just a bad idea. I think it was bred in him out of necessity during his youth.

Savannah's Dad knew from the moment I tripped on the landing walking through his front door that warm Sunday morning and Rio fell ass over end into the deep end of his pool that I'd be his roommate. Even though I ultimately walked out that day and told him I just didn't think it would work out.

I should have known better if simply for the way he immediately dove in after Rio as she was sinking, that somewhere, subconsciously, something felt right about his desire to help.

I'd already put a deposit on my very own place and not having known the man longer than a day, I was cynical. Plus, I was ready to have my very own set of keys. But, Savannah's Dad was not settling with that response, so he spent a good twenty-four hours convincing me of the fact that his solution would be the perfect transition.

"Look at it this way," he told me, "it's like getting to spend four months at a furnished vacation home, treat it like a hotel, a place that will give you a little time to figure out what you want to do next."

I couldn't deny the math, $1000 a month, an ocean view, a pool in my backyard, a guy who was never around, and his supernatural dog, who would keep my own fur-children busy and take some of the burden off me.

Still I kept struggling with the fact that I had only just stood on my own two feet. But after a short lived deliberation I gave in to the obvious and I agreed to move in on the condition that I got the front bedroom and a private area for my desk where I could do my writing.

In the weeks before I moved in he sent some of the sweetest emails I've ever been sent in my life. He promised the move would be smooth. He vacuumed my room, washed the sheets in the spare bedroom for my parents, and after he got word of my overnight at the ER he sent an email saying had I already been in the house he would have taken care of me.

But I didn't want to be taken care of. Within the first forty-eight hours I had observed that he was looking for the quiet sorts, the type of gal who would stay hidden from his "busy-gave-himself-an-ulcer" life but appear when he wanted an ear.

I'm the type of girl, who right in the middle of a story would challenge his theories, not to be rude, but because I cared enough to ask some clarifying questions. And I'm too smart to settle for the standard line that people generally feed others on their life and emotion. I listen incredibly well, and I criticize even better, and I provide just enough love in my response that you're not quite sure the difference.

My parents came to assist me with my move. Since the adjustment was tougher than I'd expected my parents stayed a few nights in the spare bedroom, until I settled in. Savannah's Dad quickly got to know me and my family at a very personal level.

Ultimately, it didn't matter that I didn't want to be taken care of, because soon after my parents left my desire to fall back into wife mode was overwhelming. I quickly found myself trotting around as "Polly Homemaker" doing dishes, cooking dinner, making him laugh when he came home stressed, and generally just making the house look, feel and smell better.

One afternoon we were talking about dating and I mentioned that I wasn't very good at the "game," he went into a nice long rant on the topic and concluded with, "You are the most down to earth, funny and caring, sweet, laughable, lovable woman I've met in a long time. Not to mention so cute you light up the room when you walk in. I don't care what kind of assholes you date, do NOT ever change. There's a guy out there who will appreciate it."

Something had caressed a previously emotionless spot in his body. But I wasn't prepared for "Hotel Americana" and I definitely wasn't ready for the life I'd just escaped. One night the inevitable discussion about boundaries ensued, emotions flew and he left. He didn't bother to come home. This was just fine by me. I was looking forward to a night alone.

At five AM the next morning I heard the gate unlatch and he came directly in my room. He waited in the doorway all of two seconds before he kicked off his shoes and climbed into my bed.

"Hi," I started plainly.

"I couldn't get home fast enough this morning," he offered sincerely.

"Sure," I responded.

"Please bare with me kid," he said as threw his arms around me in a hug. "Just a few weeks ago I was single, in a big empty house; suddenly I've got a wife, and two and a half kids."

"YOU?!" I hollered back at him with my head buried under the pillow.

"What about me?! I'm the one who just got divorced! This was supposed to be the perfect "transition home" remember?"

After that neither one of us brought it up again.

The truth of it is, we can appreciate the ambition and drive of the other, but it's the sheer fact that he's sprinting down a path that I've already trekked, and left without, that makes us want to kill each other, neither one of us made any qualms about it.

He's stressed out, financially driven, independently wealthy, and needs to chase a jaded green dollar to feel secure and wanted. Furthermore, he needs someone who admires that in him. Clearly in business or in a relationship we'd be the slow death of one another, as roommates we had assumed the role of a married couple on the outs, a ticking time bomb.

I seized his weakness as justification and began calculating a plan to move out. And while he was helping me confirm that I don't care about money or pursuing it, somewhere along the way I began to believe I could fix his one fatal flaw which confirmed that I'm still terrible at setting boundaries.

When I told Savannah's Dad the transition period was over, and it was time for me to go, he pleaded with me to stay and promised he was sorry. I'm a sucker for an apology.

The next morning he called my name from somewhere by the garage. We both share an incredible love of breakfast and there had yet to be a weekend morning where we didn't go for breakfast to share stories over eggs Benedict and two cups of coffee with extra cream for him.

I trekked across the vast house to the garage where he had the Jeep fired up in the driveway, "Hop in Kid!" he yelled.

Riding top down in a Jeep touches my heart at the very bottom, it reminds me of home and he knows it. Watching him shift gears while we sang to Kenny Rogers at the top of our lungs, drowning out the sound of the wind and each other made me question every decision I'd just made. He was a good guy, a good friend and on occasion he knew how to let loose, maybe all his stress was just a little misdirected.

Savannah's Dad reminded me that I still have a strong desire for a man who rushes home just because he knows my endless optimism and playfulness will have him smiling and laughing the minute he steps through the door.

And I taught him that while his best qualities might be intellect, wit and ambition, he needs to be secure enough to put it away for a few hours, come home after a long day put the top down and go for a cruise up the coast.

In some psychic fashion Mom must have felt my dilemma half way across the state because she called and left me this voicemail, "Remember, Michaela Renee, a lady always knows when to leave."

No matter how convenient my living arrangement might have been, I'm not here to fix him. I can't put a price on my own set of keys. It's time I unlock the front door to the future I've put in front of me, face it head on and accept it.

Savannah woke up and came to my bedside, her eyes begged for love and she gently shut them as her tail fell into a rhythmic thump. I offered up everything I had in the way of love at that insane hour of the morning. Through my half open eyes I caught a glimpse of her bloody wound, a result of an accident earlier in the week that was half my fault. I wasn't sure how I'd let her get hurt, and I wasn't quite sure how I'd walk away from her. Without either of us saying a word we exchanged immense feelings of adoration.

Just hours before Savannah's Dad had watched from across the room as I shed tears writing in my journal. He pulled Savannah close and whispered in her torn ear that it was going to go down one of two ways, either we'd fall in love and get married, or we'd be the best of friends forever. Deep down I wondered if it would be neither.

As I kissed her cold nose I told her she would be okay. I'm sure Savannah's Dad will continue to learn the lesson that Savannah speaks without saying.

NOT READY TO MAKE NICE

In 1997 I wrote a piece of work for my journalism class that was picked up by the <u>Sacramento Bee</u>, the title was, *"Who can you trust, find out the hard way."* I met my husband three months after that article was published. I was seventeen years old, this is an excerpt taken directly from the article.

> *"Everyone wants and deserves respect. If we did unto others as we'd have done to ourselves, then not so many people would feel violated by someone every day. Giving people that much, treating them as humans, can make such a difference."*

It was September and I'd spent the last year of my life learning valuable lessons, there was one thing I knew, both of us walked away from our marriage knowing that for ten years we had a solid, trusting relationship. Neither one of us ever gave the other a reason to question actions or motives of our relationship together.

Being married at such a young age was no easy task, but we both took temptation head strong and kept open lines of communication, fortunately neither of us ever had to endure the pain I heard friends speak of when it comes to lack of trust.

There's something powerful about the reciprocity of trust when it comes to relationships, especially friendships. Reciprocity in marriage and in divorce is probably the sole reason that at the end of my ten-year relationship with my ex we are able to have some respect.

"Trust" as defined by <u>Merriam Webster</u> is:

1. assured reliance on the character, ability, strength, or truth of someone or something

My character was called on the line by Tennessee, who I'd known for three years, but had only really gotten to know well during the aftermath of the divorce. While I was surrounded by friendships I'd had for years and years, this friendship blossomed quickly and came on strong and it consumed my life, my other friendships were completely overshadowed.

She felt an incredible self entitlement to the happenings in my life. As a friend, I couldn't say I blamed that. She also felt more entitled to my time than I did, and as a friend I had been willing to give that. But then I got stuck in the middle of a war zone between Tennessee, my supposed best friend, and Savannah's Dad, my roommate. Being in the middle of that sort of predicament inevitably ends with hurt and disappointment for all parties, but usually everyone's character manages to walk away in tact.

Since she couldn't confront Savannah's Dad about the fall out they'd had, she decided to take it out on me and in fairness I was an easy target. When I received the first of many slanderous text messages my natural instinct was to respond viciously back, but the truth was, I was afraid of her.

My lack of response afforded me a second round of myriad derogatory text messages. I finally received one that sent me over the edge. Terms such as "deceit" and "stretching the truth" were tossed around like a beach ball in the wind.

Words mean everything to me, and hurtful ones are not taken lightly.

I'd seen her in action, in rampage against others when she feels betrayed. Which I'd come to learn was only a response to her overwhelming sense of self entitlement. Knowing this about her helped me sit back, take a breath, look at the situation and ultimately agree with her feelings.

I tend to fall into a trap of wanting to please everyone all the time. I realized that in an effort to not hurt her, I had managed to completely evade the truth.

At some point when I first moved in with Savannah's Dad she probably did have somewhat of a right to feel entitled. But, in more ways than she was entitled, she crossed the line and overstepped her boundaries removing her right to dictate or control the situation. I continued to evaluate her accusations.

"Deceit" as defined by <u>Merriam Webster</u> is slightly more complicated:

> 1. *ensnare* 2. *to be false to or fail to fulfill* 3. *obsolete*
> 4: *to cause to accept as true or valid what is false*
> *or invalid* 5. *to while away intransitive verb: or*
> *practice <u>deceit</u>; also: to give a false impression*

I reread the different definitions and realized a few things, the first of which is that every single person has probably committed an act of deceit as it's defined under the five choices at some point, and some probably many times throughout their lives.

During the course of my friendship with Tennessee I had started to realize that intrinsically we were very different. I had a hard time relating to and accepting her behavior in various circumstances. It started to weigh on me. Frankly, I didn't have the cojones to stand up to her. Unfortunately for me, lucky for Sarita, it was a lifelong issue that I repeatedly fell akin to.

So rather than address it head on, I worked around it. I attempted to create distance in a very politically correct way. First, because amongst all the other emotional things I was coping with, I wasn't sure how to handle it. Second, because she bit with a vengeance when she was upset and I would end up backing down, suppressing my true feelings, and running away like a kicked puppy. And lastly, because I cared enough about her not to lay the truth on her.

That was my mistake, I owned it. Was I deceitful? I sure was, by literally every definition Merriam Webster offers up.

I ensnared the belief that I didn't owe it to her to make it right for once

I failed to fulfill my responsibility to her as a friend to tell her the issues I had with her

I accepted that it would be okay to let her continue on wallowing in her self pity, when I knew her self pity was fabricated and false

I gave a false impression that everything was honkey dorey when everything had not been honkey dorey since before we left on vacation to Mexico

There was no excuse. I was guilty of utter and complete deceit in every sense of the word. At some point I convinced myself I didn't want to make it right anymore. Honestly, I didn't think I'd owed it to her after how she had behaved. Rather than just tell her I drug her along for fear of hurting her. I should have told her that our friendship was hanging by a thread and I needed time and space to repair it. I couldn't find the strength to tell her to quit deciding what was right for me (that's my burden) and to quit judging me. At the end of the day I knew the only person who should be stumbling around in my flip-flops was me.

Ultimately, all my acceptance of deceit was fine. The real question was by the definition of trust, did my actions redefine my character?

Did my behavior make years of fantastic friendships, a ten year trusting relationship with my ex, and being a general caregiver to all things human and animal null and void?

Ultimately, with gut wrenching-chest in a knot-head racking confusion, I found the ability to breathe. While I may have messed up, I was still a good person. I slept soundly knowing I wasn't the first person to encounter this. At the young age of seventeen I was writing about trust, and some ten years later I was still talking about it, the Dixie Chicks said it best with their song, "I'm not ready to make nice."

Rather than flatter her, I decided to create space and distance and avoid the conversation entirely. Sarita helped me put it into perspective; some people come into our lives for a period of time to help us decide which way to walk when we come to an intersection in our path. Sometimes that person joins us for our walk, but sometimes we part ways at the crosswalk, to no fault of the other.

I thanked Tennessee for what she gave me, and mostly what she taught me, and naturally she did not take to that well. She had become accustomed to getting her way. Ending the friendship was the first step toward teaching me I had the right to stand up for what I believed in, and walk away from what I didn't.

ONLINE BLOG MID SEPTEMBER 2008
A NEW PERSPECTIVE

There were a few days that I was crushed. Good or bad I really started believing I'd lost a lot more than I'd gained moving in with Savannah's Dad. That was until the night Sarah Palin gave her big speech.

I'd gone for a beach run with Rio to clear my head from the blow I'd had to my gut from the fall out with Tennessee. When I got home he had the TV tuned into the Republican National Convention, and it was cranked up loud, I'm pretty sure half of La Jolla could hear it.

I went into the kitchen and quickly cooked some wheat pasta with marinara and tossed a salad for both of us. I poured myself a glass of Pinot Grigio and him a glass of water. When I called out to him that dinner was ready he was so intently glued to the television that I ended up bringing it over to him and we ate dinner on our laps, sitting across from each other on the L-shaped couch waiting to see what she'd say for herself.

In fairness Palin's speech was pretty impressive, I'd not known her from Adam, and I found her quite entertaining. When the speech was over, I had barely popped the last crouton into my mouth when he launched into politics.

A topic I enjoy tossing around, but don't really care to dive into after only a single glass of wine. Not to mention, he's obsessed with John McCain. Matter of fact, I don't think McCain's wife loves and supports him as much as this guy.

During the entire time I'd lived with him I don't think I've seen him so passionate about something, ever.

So I humored him simply because I was impressed by his incredible excitement and enthusiasm. The conversation began with Palin's speech and what it meant for Republicans and Democrats. His idea of a conversation is him talking, and me listening, without a single interruption. Before long he's delving into rhetorical questions about Barack Obama and the government and so on and so forth.

About ten minutes in I finally interrupted with a clarifying question. Big no-no.

"KID! There's something you NEED to understand. I'm going to get to everything you could possibly think of to ask me. If you'd just shut up for a second and let me finish."

Waiting for him to get to the punch line in a joke, or get to the point in any conversation, is like waiting for Israel and Iraq to come to terms on the conflict. And I've never been accused of being the most patient individual.

I knew him well enough though to know this time he was very serious. So I bit my tongue, held my lip and took a deep breath. That lasted about another ten minutes or so, but after about a good twenty minutes I was tired of being talked at. So in my journalistic, make-them-squirm, Barbara Walters-esq questioning technique, I began to challenge his position on the topic.

Within a matter of moments we were revving the engines headed for a full on debate. The pace car had pulled off the track and we were dropping into second gear. The kicker of it is, I really didn't have a strong opinion either way. By then I was just debating for the sole purpose of making him understand there are in fact two sides to every argument.

I continued to question his train of thought. He just didn't take that well, because his train was the only one pulling through Grand Central Station tonight. He got incredibly loud and more pissed off than I thought was humanely possible.

He was literally trembling and shaking. He wasn't going to quit until I rolled over and agreed to vote for McCain. I have never ever seen someone get so upset in my life. For a moment I was zapped to another place and time, and slowly from experience, I started to shut down systematically.

All of a sudden he catapulted from the couch towards the kitchen. I was terrified. I watched from some place outside of my body as he threw open the fridge and yanked out the Trader Joes Apple Juice. He poured himself a glass and started pacing the kitchen.

I sat silently watching.

"Oh sure, NOW you SHUT UP," he yelled. "Go ahead! You wanted to talk so bad. Speak then!"

I stayed silent.

"WHAT?" he screamed.

"I'm just waiting for it," I said.

"WAITING FOR WHAT?" he demanded.

Then all of a sudden it clicked in his head. It'd been ten years since someone had been so violently upset with me and not acted out.

I watched as he set the glass of apple juice on the counter, and immediately headed straight for me. I took a deep breath and leaned back as he narrowed the space between us. He knelt down on the floor in front of me and took both of my hands in his. He looked directly in my eyes with incredible warmth and said, "I would never, ever, hit a woman. I would NEVER hurt you, no matter how upset I am."

I guess it was all my nervousness, adrenaline and memories wrapped up into one big ball of emotion, because all of a sudden I did the oddest thing. I started laughing hysterically.

"Are you laughing at me now?" he questioned.

"I'm laughing WITH you!" I joked.

"But I'm NOT laughing," he pointed out.

I got up and started to clean up the dishes and he took out the trash and let the girls out for one last pee before bedtime. We split in the hallway to head for our separate rooms. As I brushed my teeth I replayed the events from the night. After spitting a wad of frothy Colgate in the bottom of the sink, I knocked on his door and called his name.

A millisecond later he was standing in the door way in his pajamas waiting for what I was about to say.

I just threw my arms around him. He grabbed back in a firm hug. Just the night before he defended my name to Tennessee, my ex-best friend, and now he'd done the unthinkable. After ten years of believing the wrong way was the only way, we shared an experience that showed me it doesn't always have to end like that.

As I lay in bed that night laughing over the visual of him pacing the kitchen like a lion behind bars at the zoo, I knew that everything was exactly as it was meant to be. The events that unfolded in the prior forty-eight hours were the sole reason I had endured living there for six weeks in state of confusion.

I had a new perspective, I didn't cause the anger or the pain, and I couldn't have stopped it, I just got in the way. My transition was officially done and seven days later I moved out.

LE CREUSET & THE VUNDERHOUND

In the first few weeks after we filed for divorce my ex-husband and I had found ways to live apart. But, eventually I blew through all eighty-thousand of my Marriott points, and had come home to face the music even though the dance was done.

I had cordoned myself off upstairs and he stayed downstairs. We were both miserable. There was no way either of us could start the healing process under the same roof. He shared in heartfelt honesty that he couldn't live alone in the big ole house that used to be our home and face the problems or the shadows lurking around every corner. If I didn't have to worry about uprooting the dog and the cat I would have already been long gone.

It was cold, and I was still lying in bed attempting to sort through the shambles of my life. I heard him heading up the stairs. I heard him pause, then he knocked on the wall in the stairwell, it was the rule we'd established to give me some privacy. I hesitated a moment and told him to come on up, a suggestion I quickly regretted. The door creaked slightly ajar and the cat jumped off my bed to head over to him. He plopped down on the floor directly in front of the door, picked up the cat and began sobbing.

It wasn't the first morning I'd woken up to the sound of his sobs in the hallway since the process of divorce had begun, but today my heart was weak. Throughout our entire lives together, from the time I was seventeen and he was nineteen years old; I'd been the one keeping us on key. When the chords didn't progress I went back to the writing tablet, staying strong for both of us. This morning was different, the song had ended, the stations were broadcasting static, and I couldn't listen to it anymore.

I got out of bed and walked toward the bathroom. He was tucked in a fetal position with his arms clutching his knees, rocking back and forth, shaking his head and crying. Slowly I was dying. I brushed my teeth and headed for the walk-in closet to change. I took an extra long time and still ended up with an outfit that didn't match, my hair was a mess. I didn't look much better than I did when I rolled out of bed. I finally gave up and came out of the closet, he was still there.

I pulled strength from somewhere deep inside to step over him and tell him that someday he would be okay. With that I left him in a ball of tears on the landing of our two-story home.

I loaded up the dog, got in the car and drove north. I wasn't sure why. I was going nowhere, but I was getting there fast. In the car I could crank up the radio and drown out the morning. Jennifer Nettles was having a hard time matching my volume as I sang "Somethin More" at the top of my lungs. I successfully held my tears at bay until I hit Del Mar.

It had always been our dream to make wise real estate transactions so that we could purchase that home off of Del Mar Heights road, the little beige one with the view that just needed some love. As I approached the exit I made a fist, clutched that dream, rolled down the window and let my hand get whipped back by the wind. As I passed the exit I unraveled my fingers and watched that dream fly away.

I kept driving until I reached Palomar Airport Road, and turned off. I needed gas. As I filled up the fourteen gallon tank I saw the sign for the Carlsbad Premium Outlets. Since I was quite depressed by this point; I figured a little retail therapy would do me some good.

I immediately found parking up front, which always indicated it would be a good shopping day and started trolling around the mall. I was praying Rio wouldn't drop an after breakfast load of pooh on the sidewalk. That's when I stumbled onto Le Creuset.

I must have looked downright pathetic, in my non-color coordinated thrown together outfit with the dog around my waist peeking through the clear glass window into the high end French kitchen store. But a sales clerk, an older gentleman, came to the door anyway.

"We're dog friendly; would you like to come in?"

I nodded.

"Is this a GREYHOUND?" he asked excitedly.

"She's more like a VunderHound," I offered the standard line pronouncing "Wonder" in my best German accent, "but yes, she's a retired racer from Tucson."

"Does the VunderHound know how to sit?" he asked as he extended her a dog treat.

"She not only sits, but she shakes, she's shy, she knows bang, she can be "coyote ugly" and she'll even take a bow at the end."

I proceeded to request Rio perform her tricks and she delivered. He was incredibly impressed with the final bow I'd taught her and jaunted off to tell the other employees about Rio the VunderHound.

I continued deeper into the store with her on a tight lead as I tippy toed around the displays; it'd be just my luck that her prehensile tail would knock over some beautiful over-priced ceramic dish and the VunderHound would quickly be demoted to filthy dog.

I found myself staring at the gorgeous display of flame, green and yellow Le Creuset serving dishes, remembering the day at the outlets in Palm Springs when I first saw them.

I had begged my husband to let me bring the salt and pepper shakers home. It was a holiday weekend and they were on sale-twenty percent off. But he just didn't see the value; he hated the color, the funky retro handles and the price.

The older gentleman must've sensed my dilemma, or maybe it was because I still hadn't taken my sunglasses off my face for fear of exposing the swollen puffy red patches of eyelids where my green eyes used to be, because he headed over and paused behind me.

"So, what brings you and the VunderHound into Le Creuset today?"

I gave the shortest explanation I had, "Honestly, the answer to that is quite lengthy and I'm not sure after twenty minutes of rambling I'd come to any logical conclusion except to say that I've wanted these for a very long time, and my husband, er, ex-husband would never let me purchase them. So after a very long morning I find myself cruising up the Interstate 5, quite literally tossing my dreams out the window and staring into your store at a new dream."

"Like Martin Luther King!" he exclaims.

I began laughing, and said, "Exactly! I have a dream! I have a dream, that someday I will have my very own place, with no bad memories and with no tears. My very own happy little home, and in it, I will have these salt and pepper shakers."

With that he began sharing his eerily similar story. He asked me to believe him when he said that sooner than later my heart would be healed, that we'd both be on our new journey with no regrets, and that I would be happy and confident with my new life.

Even though we were very different people, on incredibly different life paths, there was a bond between us. I believe that everyone we meet, we meet for a reason. He was no exception.

"I really appreciate hearing you say that, because days like today I'm just not so sure." I continued partly feeling sorry for myself and partly feeling guilty about his sales tactic. "While I'd really like to purchase both of these, I will hold out hope and will only purchase the olive oil and vinegar in the flame color today."

"A sweet girl like you deserves both. I expect you'll be back sooner than you know for those salt and pepper shakers, and when you do, I'll be here."

I considered that he was retired and figured he'd probably kick it before I'd be back to purchase those shakers, but as he escorted me to the register I told him he had a deal.

I brought home the olive oil and vinegar containers, and life went on. My ex husband moved out shortly thereafter, eventually the house sold, and I moved into the furnished temporary house with Savannah's Dad. While I didn't bring much to the Mount Soledad house with Savannah's Dad I did bring the olive oil and vinegar containers and my rusty, old, glass salt and pepper shakers.

And when I finally left Savannah's Dad's I had the keys to my new apartment in one hand and the olive oil and vinegar containers in the other. It wasn't long before I got a text from him:

Of all the shit you could have left, you left me the rusty salt & pepper shakers?

I chuckled considering he didn't know the half of it. I'd been in my new apartment seven days; I'd already picked out paint colors, and unpacked every box. The olive oil and vinegar looked lonely next to the stove by themselves, and tomatoes just aren't the same without a light-artery clogging salt dust.

It was a warm Saturday afternoon in San Diego, I was sweaty and exhausted from having been outdoors at a concert for the better half of the day, but it was getting late and I still had some business to take care of.

I'd been to the Carlsbad Premium Outlets for retail therapy at least ten times during the last year, but I'd never once tempted myself with Le Creuset, though I definitely did some damage over at the Coach store a time or two.

As I pulled off at the Palomar Airport Road exit I realized just how nice it felt that I didn't have anyone to check in with, no husband, no roommate, no one. For the first time in my life I was taking care of me, and it felt good.

I didn't really have any expectations as I pulled in the parking lot, but I did land a spot right up front. I snapped Rio's leash around my waist, caught my smelly, messy reflection in my car window, stood up tall and walked proudly toward the back of the mall.

Rio naturally took her fourth crap of the day right on the sidewalk. I still managed to keep my head high as I did my best to scrape the runny pooh off the cement and continued on my way to Le Creuset with disapproving looks searing the back of my head. As I reached the door I paused momentarily to let Rio do her after pooh pee. I didn't need any accidents.

All of sudden I heard, "It's HER!"

I looked up to see the older gentleman headed my way. He gently grabbed my arm and pulled me inside the store. "See!" he started announcing my entrance to all patrons of the store, "It's her! Watch this, she bows. Can you have her bow? I told her you'd be back, she didn't believe me." he said to another clerk.

I knew very well that Rio hadn't peed yet and admittedly, I was startled. But I was also teary and smiling. I've never received such a warm welcome in my life. The woman, another sales clerk in her 40's, was waiting patiently.

"Rio, can you take a bow?" I requested. And Rio immediately curtsied. The employees proceeded into a round of applause, which I'm pretty sure was for the VunderHound, but I still felt like it was partly for me.

It had been almost a year. And he'd waited. He launched into the story and the woman who had been hired shortly after I'd bought the olive oil and vinegar containers kept barging in to add her pieces of the fairytale. "Some shattered girl comes in one day, and promises she'll be back for some salt shakers (yeah right), a year goes by and then voila! Here she is! A strong confident woman and she really does have a VunderHound that bows!"

We walked over to the display and I'm still shaking my head in disbelief when he says, "And now we face the only dilemma you have left in life today..." he pauses for effect, "the flame to match the olive oil and vinegar or the green salt and pepper shakers to compliment?"

The choice was easy. Because life was simple, I'd lost it all, and gained everything, all at the same time. As I left they made me promise to come back soon and give them updates. I obliged and they knew I'd keep my word. Besides there was no shortage of great things to purchase at Le Creuset in

257

the event that a woman and her VunderHound need a little retail therapy.

As soon as we got outside Rio squatted right in the planter out in front of the door. I suddenly remembered how long she'd been holding it and she'd even been performing her tricks a few times over for each store employee. I bent down and planted a kiss on her long snout and told her that she truly is the VunderHound.

A CROCK OF HORSE POOH

It was early October, all of the boxes from storage were unpacked and I had settled into my new apartment very nicely. All the boxes except a rather enormous box of books that weighed about 4,000 pounds. Despite the fact that I'd moved twice, and didn't need or want to be spending money on more furniture I had to go buy a bookshelf.

I finally found one that would hold all my books, go with the rest of the décor, and look nice as well. There was just one problem. It came in a box. This terrified me. But I was determined to be independent! I had already purchased my very own drill and hung all my artwork on my own, so the bookshelf project should be a simple task. I managed to get the huge box out of the store and into my apartment all by myself.

The documentation that came with it said:

> *Congratulations! You've just purchased a fine furniture item. We have designed our furniture with you in mind. Our clear, easy to follow, step by step instructions will guide you through the project from start to finish.*

Feel confident that this will be a fun and rewarding project. The final product will be a quality piece of furniture that will go together smoothly and give years of enjoyment.

All you will need is a Phillips screwdriver and a hammer.

So I placed a little call to the documentation writers at Linon.com.

"Um, hello. I purchased the five shelf bookshelf," I began.

"Thank you for your purchase," the kind receptionist replied.

"No, really, thank YOU. I'm calling because I just wanted to let you know that not only do I want a refund on my bookshelf, but I'd like you to send me a new hammer as well."

"I'm sorry you are requesting a refund. Can you tell me what's wrong with the product?"

"Yes, your bullshit instructions were not easy to follow, and the packet of hardware labeled A- Q was not very clear at all. I'm not sure where the years of enjoyment come into play, maybe when I invite my friends over, and they laugh their butts off at my pathetic attempt at building a bookshelf.

I followed the step by step instructions, word for word, but somehow I wound up with one less shelf than it shows in the picture on the box. Maybe that's because I finally found a use for the hammer you'd said I need. How handy is it that the backside of my hammer has that ax like tool to slam through the shelves when they won't snap into place?

As it would turn out you do make a pretty quality piece of furniture, because I had to hit it with the hammer like fifty times to finally get it to look right. And last but not least, if you call this fun and rewarding, I'd like to see your idea of challenging but thought provoking."

"Mam, are you through?"

"I'm not a mam, I'm a miss, and the MISS is the reason I'm building this damn shelf on my own to begin with, you want to talk about that now too?"

"Miss..."

"Yes?"

"We'll gladly take your return at any one of our San Diego locations."

ONLINE BLOG MID OCTOBER 2008
SERIES OF FORTUNATE EVENTS

I spent the latter portion of the early half of the evening instant messaging with my online friend CLaKewer who, thanks to Facebook, I can call a friend, even though we've never met face to face.

We don't have to because of the circumstances.

Through his social networking page I catch a glimpse into his life and through his status updates I gain a better understanding of who he is as a person. Plus, he's friends with "Mister Disappointment," who I've managed to establish a real-life friendship with in recent weeks, and whose general judgment of character I value. So through some tweaked version of six degrees of separation, we are friends. At least Facebook says so.

The dialogue of instant message chat is a funny one, two people each pausing, having the opportunity to backspace and retype what you really want to say. Your mind gets enough opportunity to process and correct. Not quite as much time as an email, but definitely more than on the phone or in person.

I definitely don't recommend IM chat for the highly analytical for the obvious reason that you would spend far too much time over-thinking what the other person is typing and rethinking what you should respond with. For the "oops did I just say that out loud" type, such as myself, IM chat can be a nice combination of "spit it out" and "stop and pause" plus there's always the emoticons if it's just not flowing right.

Example chat thread:

> *Dude pics of ur new girlfriend woof, she's fugly, doh ;) luv ya xoxo muah.*

Whereby, in person the conversation would sound like, "Good to see you, did I mention those pictures you mailed of your girlfriend? Wow! She's a dead ringer for my Great Grandpa once removed... Yeah, totally, same exact nose. Anyway, so glad that's working out for you." Insert real life awkward smile here.

Imagine what would happen if we lived our in person lives in IM chat speed with IM chat backspace. Take for example, "Mister Disappointment" and I sitting at sushi enjoying a meal together back in May. He drops a bomb and in real life I react. How I reacted really isn't important; be it shocked or sad or happy or confused, because immediately he sees my expression and immediately the moment can not be reversed.

Imagine if in that moment, in that second with all of the emotions creating a very specific situation, you had the opportunity to pause allowing your mind processes the consequence and then react, slowly and deliberately with the opportunity to delete before you hit send.

I might venture to say that many first kisses would be missed. That many laughs related to bad timing would be skipped. Jokes would never be created and maybe in the case of my failed marriage, he would have stopped his fist from swinging.

Likewise I would extend a reach to the concept that regrets would be worse and not better. The moments I don't regret are the ones where I reacted (yes, I said reacted) in the spur of the moment; though at the time I definitely regretted them or wished for other alternatives.

So this evening during my chat with CLaKewer, the topic of circumstance came up. I pondered this thought and realized that no instant message chat could do this topic justice. We were just about to sign off for the evening and started the online chat goodbye process with something like:

gret to finally chat w u. signing off for the nite, g'nite.

And then I felt that spur of the moment, not-quite-ready-to-say-goodbye jitters, and added a bunch of text mumbo jumbo. This would be the equivalent to the quick seconds when two friends' part ways after happy hour, knowing they've agreed to see each other soon, but another three months will likely go by before it comes to fruition.

Upon going "offline" which, since I'm always "online" is really more like "unavailable," the first thing I did was Google "circumstance."

I was nothing short of appalled at the variety of meaning and the breadth of relation the word causes; I think I may have found my new favorite word. My old favorite word is a proper noun. A name that warms my heart, sounds good rolling off my tongue and causes me to stop, pause and smile wherever I may be, regardless of whatever other proper nouns I might be enjoying happy hour with.

Think for a moment about what comes to mind when you first read the word "circumstance."

Is it a distinct memory? Is it a variety of incidences leading up to a pivotal moment? Is it a general bout of misfortune that leads to a situation? A series of fortunate events? Is it out of your control? Does Circumstance = Consequence? Does Circumstance = Fate?

Earlier on in our chat conversation I had told CLaKewer that I'd been having writers block and ironically our random, organized, fluid motion of chat talk lead me to type these words:

haha circumstance, such an odd concept.

As soon as I hit send, which was immediately after I finished typing it, I thought, what an odd word choice! I sat there staring at it, realizing I couldn't take it back even though I wanted to. That epiphany broke my writers block.

I didn't mean "circumstance!" I meant "the situation" and all the random things pertaining to the situation. Including a few examples I'd shared with him. Such as the fact that "Mister Disappointment" and I happened to be in the same airport at the same moment a few months ago; which also just so happens to be an airport in the city where CLaKewer lives.

Or that "Mister Disappointment" and I hadn't seen each other in months and just happened to find ourselves standing across an intersection from each other on a street corner in a town that I only just moved to days before, that he doesn't live in, waiting to cross at the exact same moment in each other's direction.

So why in a spur of the moment reaction did my mind type "circumstance" when that's not what I meant at all...or did I? Circumstance is rarely found on its own. This is not an accident.

There are extenuating circumstances, there is aggravating circumstances, attendant/external circumstances, exigent circumstances, special circumstances, communities of circumstance (such as action, interest, position, practice and purpose) and there is even "Pomp and Circumstance" which is a series of marches comprised for an orchestra by Sir Edward Elgar and derived of Shakespeare:

The title is taken from Act III, Scene iii of Shakespeare's Othello:

> *Farewell the neighing steed, and the shrill trump,*
> *The spirit-stirring drum, the ear-piercing fife,*
> *The Royal banner, and all quality,*
> *Pride, Pomp, and Circumstance of glorious war!"*

But I think what truly surprised me the most, is that circumstance, in and of itself, all by its lonesome, by every definition is a noun aka: person, place or thing.

And what's even more interesting, is this noun always affects something else. As a matter of fact, it does not even exist without determining and dictating the outcome of events.

This evening, my chat with CLaKewer, and the circumstance, if you will, began in March.

In March I was supposed to stay home. But instead I went out with Tennessee, who I'd only just started getting to know. Her boyfriend ends up leaving us at a bar in La Jolla to go to a house party in Del Mar (no girls allowed) and then rejoined up with us an hour later. But, somewhere in between the house party in Del Mar and the bar Tennessee and I were sitting at, he picked up some friends, "Mister Disappointment" and one other guy.

Tennessee and her boyfriend had begun fighting (because there had been girls at the party after all); I was forced due to the awkward situation to begin dialogue with "Mister Disappointment" and the other guy. Somewhere during the evening I lost sight of Tennessee, who was also my ride for the evening, and so "Mister Disappointment" found me on the dance floor and swapped cell numbers with me so that I would have a ride home if needed (sweet, I know and one of the reasons I didn't expect him to end up being such a disappointment).

Turns out I didn't need a ride, but "Mister Disappointment" ended up texting and talking anyways. Then we ended up dating anyways, and then we ended up breaking up anyways. Then I ended up posting a "blog" online (Who Doesn't Bring Wine?) about him and he ended up sharing that with one of his friends, CLaKewer.

After a long drawn out EU text message relationship "Mister Disappointment" and I made up and became "frenemies" on Facebook. I just can't seem to Shift Delete this one. Then, CLaKewer, who had enjoyed my writing, ended up adding me as a friend on Facebook in August. So this entire evening, a series of events, came to a pivotal moment when I end up instant messaging with CLaKewer about life and I realized...Well this is odd...

Through a complete and total accident, I'm chatting with someone in another state who I've never met before. But, CLaKewer is my friend, because I met him through Tennessee's boyfriend's friend, "Mister Disappointment." And what is even odder is that I no longer talk to Tennessee because of the whole Savannah's Dad incident and her and her boyfriend are no longer together. So in an instant replay today, I would never have met "Mister Disappointment" or CLaKewer if it weren't for the circumstances.

So essentially, I met Tennessee, and she met her boyfriend and her boyfriend met "Mister Disappointment," at a house party in Del Mar and "Mister Disappointment" met me, so I could meet CLaKewer on Facebook and talk about life.

Circumstance is a noun, an event accompanying, conditioning or determining another an essential or inevitable concomitant.

So I guess, technically by definition, circumstance is an accident waiting to happen. A series of events outside of your control leading to an outcome. Circumstance = Fate. Paradoxically fate is a noun too.

ONLINE BLOG LATE OCTOBER 2008
NO MORE WHAT IFS

Until Friday night, no matter what had been going on in my life, no matter how tragic the circumstances, no matter how difficult the day, my parents house had always been a place I found comfort. When I snuggled into the jersey knit sheets in the West Elm designed guest bedroom, it was home, even though I never grew up in that house. Regardless of the thoughts running rampant in my mind like a marathon runner; the smells of the pine, the chilly mountain breezes and the safe feeling of having Mom and Dad just down the hall, allowed my body to drift into a deep sleep. That is until Friday night.

I'm not sure what brought me to Georgetown this weekend. I really had no good reason, except that I had wanted to see the family. I wanted to do a little camping, sans cell phones and any connection to the real world. And, I guess I'd just missed them. I'd just sold the house and been through three moves in forty-five days, life was finally settling in and I needed a good ole fashioned family fix.

When I woke up Friday morning it was exactly like any other Friday in my trips prior. Mom called me from the patio to come out and enjoy a cup of coffee. I'd stayed up late the night before trolling through family photos and the brew smelled like the perfect wake up call. I filled the mug to the top leaving just enough room for French vanilla creamer and two Splenda's and headed out into the chill.

I was still in San Diego pajamas (tank top and snug fitting boy shorts) and the breeze struck my skin like needles. I immediately headed back inside and straight to the closet to grab Dad's oversized blue sweatshirt. I knew exactly where it was always kept and I knew exactly the warmth it offered on mornings like these.

Mom and I sat sipping coffee discussing my brother's upcoming wedding. My subconscious processed the following chain of events: Mom whistles and hollers "Max," the disconcerting roar of a raised up crew cab-dually blowing by my parents house somewhere off in the distance, and the glimmer the last ounce of sun created on the silver fur of the little stuffed toy laying on the patio stairs.

The storm was creating a dreary combination in the serene garden setting my parents had created for their backyard. Mom mentioned they planned to get the fence surrounding the property completed before my brother's ceremony.

We were talking about décor and design, as I headed through the house towards the front yard to demonstrate an idea I had aloud to Mom.

The view from my parent's patio is quite beautiful. The house is built into a hill and surrounded by one hundred years of forest growth, beautiful pine trees, and a 180° view of their property, including the big circular driveway that leads to the county-maintained, two lane curvy mountain road below.

Mom and I saw the car slow at the same time, which prompted her reaction. Her eyes began to scan the yard and she asked with a tremble in her voice, "Michaela where's Max?"

I was still staring down on the road as the car pulled away exposing his little lifeless body lying across the double yellow lines. The only explanation I have for the words I screamed next is that somehow my conscious mind had finally processed what my subconscious had already known.

Max was dead.

I didn't hesitate. I darted back through the house, out the back door and sprinted down the long driveway barefoot. I was rolling up the baggy sleeves on Dad's sweatshirt as I approached the road. I saw something blood red lying within a foot of his body. I froze.

I glanced back at Mom who was limping down the driveway on the knee she'd just had surgery on and screamed at her to get the car. My whole body wanted to run, my heart wanted to collapse in a ball with my gut where I stood. I have no idea where I found the strength to continue towards Max, but within seconds I was dropping to my knees in the middle of the road.

I immediately placed my right arm delicately under his neck and reached with my left arm for the red still lying in the road. It was his collar, it had snapped in half. I picked it up and tucked my other arm under him, one look in his eyes told me he was gone, but I didn't care. I gently stood up and told him he would be okay and swallowed back the lump in my throat that was my tears waiting to fall.

Carrying him in my arms like a child using Dad's sweatshirt for protection from the wind, I calmly repeated over and over that he was going to be okay, the SUV pulled up next to me, and Mom reached over and threw open the door and I climbed in. When we got to the animal hospital in town, they were still closed. I screamed every curse word at the top of my lungs demanding they open the door. "The doctor's not in," she responded through the glass door as she took her precious time trying to find the keys.

Mom was shaking her hands up and down and crying and I finally screamed, "I don't give a FUCK open this door right now!" I was about ready to kick it in with my foot when she finally opened it and I carried him to the operation table and gently laid him down. She reached for her stethoscope and began to listen.

As I paced back and forth, silently waiting, the nurse scanned him over and I started to process everything that had happened. Up until now I was just reacting.

Minutes before Max was not just alive, he was very alive. He had stayed up late helping me flip through the photo albums snorting with that crushed up Boston Bull Terrier nose of his. He had begged to join me, with his wet muddy feet, on the patio chair for coffee. He had tossed his silver stuffed toy in the air and left it where it lay to run off and do something else more fun because he lived life in the moment. Seconds later, I was staring down on what used to his life, holding his snapped red collar in my hands.

Seeing him on the stainless steel table at the Animal ER brought back all the horrible last moments of both Indy and Java's lives. Why did I have to be here for this?

I lost my patience and demanded the nurse tell me whether or not he had a pulse. After the passing of a lifetime she finally opened her eyes and pulled the tubes out of her ears and shook her head no.

I immediately walked outside where Mom was waiting; she was crying hysterically, I told her he was gone. She handed me her cell phone, and dropped her head in her hands, she was inconsolable. I gathered the quiver in my voice when Dad answered the line and I managed to tell him his best friend was dead.

The moment I hung up I screamed at the top of my lungs, "THIS IS NOT SUPPOSED TO GO LIKE THIS!" and began crying. The type of crying that is really more like hiccup-choking. The kind of crying I had done a lot of this year.

I drove us home from the Animal ER, I was really not okay, and Mom knew it. When she got inside the house she immediately began picking up Max's toys while retelling the story in tears to everyone who had begun calling the house. I felt the downward spiral begin.

I hadn't felt it in a long time, it's that feeling when you step off the spinning ride at the carnival, the one where you don't know whether you need to stand or sit, but you know you're about to vomit. The one where your whole body screams that it needs relief from the constant spin and the weight of your head is so heavy that even your shoulders start to drop. It's called a panic attack.

By this point Mom had begun to get toys out from under the media niche, she was lying on the floor, and she wasn't getting up. We both needed a hug but I couldn't go to her. I just couldn't do it.

She suggested I call Sarita, but I called Savannah's Dad, who was watching Rio and Dash while I was away. He answered and I was barely able to tell him what happened, "Hearing you like this is killing me," he said. "If I could have any wish right now it would be to take this pain away from you, and put it on me."

I didn't know what to say, that was just about the sweetest thing anyone had ever said to me. He told me that he would give the kids extra love tonight and told me to go check on my Mom. I hung up and called Sarita, I was dying.

After talking with her I found enough strength to go get in the shower. I stood there letting the water pour down over my arms that just minutes before had held Max's little body. As always the water washed away the tears. I was in a trance until Mom began pounding on the door to the bathroom asking me to please hurry up. She couldn't stand to be in the house any longer.

As soon as I got out of the bathroom I gave her a hug. "I needed this fifteen minutes ago, but I'll take it now," she said.

"I know Mom, I just couldn't do it."

I got in the car, which just an hour before had transported little Max. As she drove down the curvy road I stared off out the window trying to replay, while trying to forget, the morning events. Mom started talking to fill the void of silence in between us.

"Michaela, I know you don't know why you had to be here for this, but I just want you to know, I could never have done what you did today. God needed you here with me. You are stronger than you even know. This morning, I saw a woman that I've never seen before. I'll be honest, in the last few months I've worried about you. Both me and your Dad have. What I saw this morning, I needed. Now I know, no matter what happens, you will be okay. You've changed so much, so much for the better."

I didn't process what she said, I couldn't. My whole body ached and my mind was racing to process the what-ifs. Not just Max's what-if's, but my what-if's. That car ride felt like an eternity, and I hoped that someday I would find a way to reason with my mind over the events and all of the what-ifs that were haunting me.

Dad was due home any minute and Mom had asked me to please be strong for him. I tried for her. But when Dad came through the door and Max didn't greet him, he lost it. We all did. That night everyone came together to support each other like we had done many times in the past. Max truly was a part of our family. We found a way to laugh, telling stories and playing games, we found a way to continue on, which I've learned you always do.

It was Friday night when my parents headed down the hallway and I turned for the guest room. I realized that Max wouldn't be up late with me and he wouldn't be snuggling, and just as I closed my eyes I was presented with the visual of him laying lifeless in the center of the road.

What-if?

What-if I'd gotten up when Mom whistled and he didn't come? What-if I'd let him up on the patio chair to cuddle with me? What-if I had told Mom I'd rather sit inside in the warmth than outside in the chilly air? What-if I'd brought Rio with me this weekend? What-if I hadn't come at all? Mom would have been at work and Max would be alive.

The moments that separate life and death, especially when dealt in tragic circumstances, are difficult for the mind to comprehend. As mom and I sat drinking our sorrows away that day, she said, "Remember how you don't do "New Years

Day" you do "Write off day" instead? Well I'm writing off every day this whole year."

I can't write it all off. Through the pain I've learned so much. If above nothing else, 2008 taught me that life is too short and we only get one chance at it. I might not have been able to change what happened with Max, but last weekend I learned not to chance the what-ifs. What-if I didn't say I love you, when I really do? What-if I didn't send someone a card just because I was thinking about them? What-if I didn't hug tight, just a little longer because it feels right?

As I waited to board the plane on Sunday I watched the people around me coming and going, life was moving on. I wondered how many people forgot to shake hands, hug, kiss or simply smile before they left today. I walked on my plane knowing I'd hugged my parents tighter and a little longer than ever before. Life's too short, no more what-ifs.

I'LL WALK WITH WHOMEVER

All Savannah's Dad texted was:

I miss you.

That's really all it took. I'd just met up with my friend Judi for some wine therapy. It had been a week since I'd seen him, he had been trying to give me time to sort through my feelings, and give me space.

He knew it was important to me to prove to myself that I could handle my new apartment and independence. I had been trekking through the dark alleys of an unforgiving world. Slowly I had come to terms with my dashed hopes and anxiously I placed my dreams on the front line. When the text came through, I contemplated for a moment proving my resilience to someone. But to who? And why? And what for?

So instead I grabbed my car keys, but this time, unlike all the others, I closed up the windows in my apartment, the way you close them up when you know you aren't coming back for awhile.

Savannah's Dad was lying on the couch when I walked through the front door. With caution he watched from afar as I kicked off my shoes and unleashed Rio. "Do you plan to stay tonight or are you going to leave like usual?" he asked.

Part of my problem was that I didn't think we had a future together. Part of the desire to see him was that I felt a twinge of guilt for all the times he ached for comfort and I left because of my feelings for "Mister Disappointment." But mostly my naked soul was finally free and longing for him, not for forever, but for right then.

I glanced up at him from the floor where my bare feet had been struck by the cold tile and said, "If you'll have me, I'd like to stay."

"I always want you to stay, come over here and get warm," he replied.

Later that evening as I laid down on his chest to tuck in for the night I realized he was comfortable, but my reasons were not. I began to question my decision to stay with him over night. It was so much easier to leave him and Savannah and go back to my companion-free comfort zone. He must've felt the increase in my heart rate because out of the dark silence he asked, "Are you going to leave in twenty minutes after I fall asleep?"

I paused to think what I had done to this man that he would even ask such a question, but he was right, that was my MO. Gently moving my hand up his bicep, my fingertips felt around for the spot in between his clavicle and his shoulder blade and when I found the muscle I tensed my fingers around it and whispered, "No, I'm not."

"Okay. Goodnight then," and within moments he was sound asleep.

I laid there while he slept and realized our breathing was synchronized, that's just how comfortable he was. Why hadn't I stayed before? Why was this night different?

I rolled over to the barren side of the bed where the sheets were still crisp and chilly and closed my eyes to replay the events that had made me grab my keys and drive to his house in the first place.

Judi and I had gone out for a glass of wine earlier in the evening and she wanted all the latest details. "You went for a walk with your ex-husband? Did Rio recognize him?" she asked as she took a sip of the dark red Pinot Noir.

I sat quiet, becoming suddenly very interested in my fizzy white Gwertz, because the truth is, my ex-husband had become Rio's past and she didn't recognize him. But I didn't know how to admit it.

Judi scanned my expression for the answer and when she found it she offered up an understanding response, "Its okay…she always was a Momma's girl. She's been through a lot too, at the end of the day, as long as you're with her, she's thinking, I'll walk with whomever."

It was an epiphany moment, which I seemed to have a lot of. Not only was Rio a Momma's girl, but she took after me too. She had no expectations for the future, only hopes. She had no thoughts of the long haul, she lived in the minute, and she wished for love but sought comfort in the moment. She's just like me, because if you hand over my leash for an hour, I'll walk with whomever too.

So I finally gave Judi an explanation, "It had been over three months since I'd seen my ex and I asked him to join me for the walk. With the turn of the winter weather and the daylight savings darkness, my heart was seeking solace. Since it was getting dark early I suggested Mission Bay which has a lighted path. I also had Savannah with me and since Savannah is a terror on the leash I opted to walk her and handed Rio's leash over to him."

"That must've been tough," Judi interjected.

"He took Rio's leash and looked at her intently. Then he knelt down and sadness swept over him. He said she didn't know him. I told him not to be silly, of course she knew him. But he was right, she didn't. Furthermore, she didn't care, so long as I was with her, and she was getting a stroll, she didn't care who held the leash. Maybe's she's EU," I joked.

Judi laughed.

"There was nothing between my ex-husband and I. There was no love, there was no emotion, the only thing that remained was history, and in our history we found peace. He's the only person in the world that can truly understand the heartache I feel from knowing this will be my first holiday season in years spent without him, because he feels it too."

"Wow, that's pretty intense," Judi responded.

"The thing is, neither one of us wanted to change it. Neither one of us would have it any other way. I'd gotten the answers I had needed. I cleared my head and in order to bring my future to the forefront, I emptied my mind of the past. He was nothing more than a walking memory. But somehow knowing we shared that history, made it better."

"What did he think of Savannah?" Judi asked.

As we parted in the shadows of the tree in the park he handed Rio back and thanked me for the walk. "Well," I began, "he said that even though Rio didn't recognize him, it was neat to see her with Savannah. And that was it. I left Mission Bay and winded up through the hills of Mount Soledad to take Savannah back home."

As I sat there sipping my white wine I thought about how many walks Rio and I'd been on, how many people we'd encountered. The many places we'd been and how many times I'd handed her leash to a friend, a date, a stranger or otherwise.

"Did you see Savannah's Dad when you dropped off Savannah?" Judi probed.

"No. I pulled in the driveway and struggled to keep Rio in the car while getting Savannah out, their leashes were intertwined. When I left Savannah I told her goodbye for awhile, I had convinced myself that I needed a break from them. I felt like it was confusing the girls, and him and I. I need to do things on my own for awhile."

"When was the last time you saw him?" she asked.

"A week ago." I ended.

One week I had been walking Rio alone, I was enjoying the freedom of a clear mind and the gratification of solitude. In seven days I came to appreciate all that was, and is, and at the end of seven days I was secure. I could walk alone, and that was ok.

Judi and I finished our glasses and I went back to my lonely apartment and all Savannah's Dad texted was:

I miss you.

Right then, I would have walked with whomever, wherever, but this time…I wasn't walking away from him.

I texted:

I miss you too.

Then I grabbed my keys and drove across town.

I felt him suddenly shift and the weight of his arm fall over my hips. I opened my eyes to watch him re-embrace my body. He used his toned arms as a gigantic ice cream scoop and shifted my lower half closer to his torso. As I felt his breath on my neck I realized that I trusted him, and I'd handed him my leash. It wasn't forever, quite the contrary, it was only for tonight, and I knew the next day I would walk alone.

ONLINE BLOG MID NOVEMBER 2008
I LOVED ALONE

I loved him, perhaps too deeply. Have you ever loved so much it hurt? I've been asked too many times why I stayed for so long. Why I didn't leave and why I endured the pain time and time again. It was because I loved him.

I'm not sure that love ever truly goes away. I think it gets tucked in a safe place in our hearts, because when we are weak and when we hurt, our mind can go to that place and reach in, and pull out a tiny bit of that love and hand it to our soul.

Love is a blessing, and love is a curse. I truly believe that those of us, who are so greatly loved, are able to love the deepest. And when I love, I love intently.

Love is the reason I stayed, and love is the reason I left him.

I've been loved, and I am loved, and while I can't lie that it still hurts like hell sometimes I'm so lucky to have had that man in my life. Even though the pain was real, the love was so much greater.

While his words cut like a knife and his fist stung, like running through a hail storm in winter, at the end of a very long day, he was still my husband and his touch became soft. If thoughts clouded my complicated mind he'd still let me rest my head on his heartbeat, gently squeezing my shoulders until I fell asleep.

To be in the company of love, I'd be willing to endure those tears. In the end I've learned to cry alone, I've learned to fall asleep alone, and I've learned that sometimes you love alone.

It was cold for October, I was wearing shorts, a t-shirt and a sweatshirt. I probably should have had on pants. The three-mile Mission Bay walk was supposed to be a good thing, a chance for us to talk through some of our issues. About one mile in, I started to realize it was bigger than me; the conversation was deeper than I could maneuver.

I continued down the paved path with Rio's leash attached loosely around my waist while he rambled on about how much he didn't like the counseling, how he didn't like Sarita, and how he thought I was the one with the problem.

"Look, after Indy and Java died, it's like you just went away," he started.

I interjected, "No, after Indy and Java died I needed you more than ever. I needed my husband to be there, to help me, and he was gone."

"You turned cold Michaela, it's like you are dead to me," he finished.

"Dead to you? Well maybe if you could control your temper every once in awhile I would care. Maybe if I wasn't so afraid of what was coming next then I would be able to turn some of my heart back on. I beg you not to do it and then I beg you not to do it again, and again. You don't give a crap, it's like you don't care, so I'll be honest, I'm finding it really hard to love you right now."

"Oh, so you admit it? You admit that you aren't in this!"

"I never left this! That's why I'm here right now trying to work through this, and why every time you say it's the last time and it's not, I still stay here. I am in this! I'm in this with you! No one would put up with this the way I do! NO ONE!"

We were getting loud, it was late, it was dark and the park had emptied out. Rio knew the rise in our voices and she started to back up. I glanced down to re-adjust her leash and by the time I looked up our heated conversation had turned to fire. His arms were around my biceps gripping tighter and tighter until I could feel my pulse flowing through the blood in my arms.

"Put up with what? Huh? Put up with what? You basically just said you checked out! What the hell do you want from me? To keep trying to love a cold hearted bitch, who won't tell me when she's upset? Who doesn't give me a chance to fix it?"

He shook me violently, his lips were only an inch from my nose, and I could feel his hot air on my face. I began to cry, "Please, we're in public, please. I'm begging you. Don't do this here. Not now."

And with that he lifted me up off the paved path and threw me down. I landed on Rio as I came crashing down into the mud. My knees were bloody, my palms were skinned, my shorts were covered in mud and my husband was running away, in the general direction of our house. One glance at the empty park told me no one had seen. It was a short lived minor outburst. I was used to much worse. I took a moment to say a little prayer for that.

I stood up and brushed the blood off my knees and looked at Rio, she was fine but acting timid. I had no cell phone, I had no car keys. He was gone, I was alone and the last place I wanted to go was home. But I did, because he was my husband and helping him work through it is what I was supposed to do, because I loved him. And rather than find some place to sleep alone; I'd rather crawl into bed with him and believe I could make it better. The only difference was his chest wasn't the safe place it used to be.

And in the dark eerie silence of our bedroom from my lonely side of our bed I whispered, "YOU need therapy."

"What are you talking about? WE'RE in therapy."

"I can't go on like this. I'm not strong enough. I can't fix this, I can't fix you, I can't fix us."

And we both started crying.

"It's the only way, please say you'll go."

I loved and he loved, but it was too late. It would only get worse, I would cry alone, I would sleep alone, and in the end I would love alone.

CLEARLY CONFUSED

Thanksgiving was just around the corner, a time to give thanks and a time to be with family. I never thought I would have kids, until I met "Mister Disappointment" and realized that there might be a man out there, that I could love, that would make a great dad. My soon to be sister-in-law called me up one morning all excited about this little baby test that her and my brother had done with the same result.

The myth is that you take a pendant necklace and swing it over your palm and it will tell you how many kids you are having and what the sex will be. You raise the necklace over your palm and it either swings side to side, in a circle, or not at all. You repeat the process until the necklace doesn't move. She went onto explain that both her and my brother did it and got a circle motion, then the side to side, and then nothing at all. According to the baby test they are having two children, the circle means they are having a girl, the side to side means they are having a boy and the final stillness predicts only those two children.

She suggested I try the test, but I was pretty convinced I wasn't having children, or was I? Furthermore, now that I thought that maybe I someday could with the right man, what did I really hope for the necklace test? I was scared and figured I didn't need to add fate to the choice equation. So instead I joked with her that I'd pull out this little lucky charm on first dates and if things didn't swing the right way, then I'd split the bill and bail.

I sat there pondering fate versus choice and as if on queue Savannah's Dad beeped in with a text message. His family was coming into town and I needed to pick up my laundry before they got there. I wasn't going to be meeting them, and we'd been arguing about it. He supposedly wasn't introducing them to anyone because, to be frank, they just weren't as cool as my parents.

The text read:

Things that need to be done while you're at the house: Make the bed, rinse down the bathroom sink, bring sheets for futon and make it, clean dog pooh.

EXCUSE ME? Who did he think I was, and what had our relationship come to?

It wasn't just a booty call, because my friends explained those only occur generally after eleven PM on weekends and you must be drunk. It wasn't just friends with benefits because sometimes he would grab my face and kiss me the way you do when you're in love. We weren't exclusive boyfriend and girlfriend because we were dating other people. And we definitely weren't married, though having lived together sharing household chores, and taking turns caring for Savannah and Rio during weekends definitely thrust us into that definition.

In this moment, I simply felt like the housekeeper who wasn't good enough to meet his family, all I needed was the French maid outfit they sell at Fredericks.

So I texted back:

EFF YOU

And within two minutes the phone was ringing.

"Look, I'd do this for you as a friend," he said.

"We're not friends," I spit coldly.

"What are we then?"

"I don't know and I don't want to discuss this anymore."

"I don't understand why you are so upset."

"That's the whole problem."

"Michaela, can you please do me this one favor and make the bed?"

"That's all you have to say for yourself? Please make the bed?"

"Look, you're just upset because you know I'm right, you know I'd do it for you…"

I hung up. I was *so* done.

Once again I grabbed my keys and sped the whole way from Del Mar to Mount Soledad. I ran around the house like a maniac collecting my personal belongings. I even took my floaties out of the pool. As a final kicker I went into the garage and "stole" my mountain bike. Which he was supposed to have tuned up and delivered to my apartment the week before.

Once I got the bike positioned next to my car I realized I had placed quite the challenge in front of me. I stared at the dilemma which was not unlike all the others in my life; I had rightfully taken a rusty, desperate looking, greasy, awkward hunk of junk. And I was attempting to cram it in a miniscule space in order to get it home with the hopes of fixing it to the point where it was actually useful for something in my life.

I should have just left it there, but I was determined. After twenty-five minutes of playing Tetris with the handlebars, the seat, and the pedals I finally figured out how to take the front wheel off. VOILA!

Without further adieu, (as if the complete workaholic was suddenly going to come home at ten o'clock in the morning) I crammed it in the back seat of my Mercedes Benz and threw the wheel in the trunk. Then I grabbed Rio, folded her up like a pretzel and equally stuffed all sixty-seven pounds of her in the front seat. She looked over at me with the same expression she gives the vet when they stick the thermometer up her rear at the hospital. "Look. I'm not having any of this from you right now!" I told her aloud, "just deal with it!"

She glanced back at the bike occupying the back seat and then back at me through the passenger window. I swear if she could speak she would have said, "Have you lost your mind?" and, "great, does this mean I can't play with Savannah anymore?" and probably, "Mom, can you just get over yourself, because Savannah's Dad is like my Dad too, even though the two of you together makes Savannah and I laugh."

I moved her tail aside and shut the door. Then I threw my shoulders back and strutted distinctly, tall and proud, to the front door. I kissed Savannah's nose and shut and locked the door. I'd been through this rigmarole before, so this time just to make it more final I took the key off my key-ring and stuck it under the mat.

I texted him:

I'm done with you. The key is under the mat.

He texted promptly back:

Did you make the bed?

That's really the crux of the whole issue. I had no inten-tion of making the bed, if for nothing other than to prove a point. Once I got inside, I was overcome by a strong emotion, one I really wasn't prepared to feel. It was a feeling of finality and misery. I wasn't prepared to experience emotion so deep for him. The strong unhappiness in the moment told me my feelings for him had been running far deeper than I'd let on. In fact, so much so that right before I left, I made his bed. Carmen yet again told me it was called "grace."

As the greasy bike and dirty dog bounced back and forth off the sides of the car through the winding roads of La Jolla I repeated to myself that we were like oil and water. Kanye West's "Love Lockdown" was blaring on my iPod. There were times I wasn't making it up, sometimes I really believed he was brain damaged, and that we'd kill each other if we attempted a relationship.

At the eleventh hour, I realized that truth be told, a few nights before, I'd started trusting him and I was clearly confused.

I suddenly felt like I was drowning. My head was working overtime attempting to convince my heart that I'd done the right thing when I received a message from CLaKewer that said:

> *Rarely does the mind work at the same speed as the heart...*

And in that moment just before you doze off to sleep, the one where you have a second to put closure to the day, I pondered what CLaKewer had said and wondered how I'd lost clarity and fallen quickly into confusion.

I began to realize that it had been much easier to obsessively love the idea of being in love with "Mister

Disappointment," who wasn't available, than be in love with the man who was.

I had spent months making a choice to intervene with the fate that I couldn't deny. I'd been making excuses for "Mister Disappointment" when I should have been giving Savannah's Dad a chance. I could come up with five hundred reasons why he didn't deserve one, but I could also come up with a thousand reasons for why he did.

I searched around for someone to blame. There was no one but myself. My actions had caused his reactions, and time and time again I made excuses and attempted to sabotage any chance of a relationship: Roommates; my feelings for "Mister Disappointment;" his intensity and financial obsessions; my free spirited nature.

Why should he introduce me to his family? Night after night I'd shoot down any chances for us on the fear that my heart would get too close when my mind didn't want to. Night after night I ran.

I had always been there for him as a lover and as a friend, but as a partner I'd failed, I'd lost his trust. Each night in that moment before I would go to sleep I would think about him and Savannah across town snoring together, and every morning I'd wonder if he made it safe to work that day.

Almost a week had gone by, since I'd left the key under the mat and I realized there was only one thing to do, quit running. I needed to be honest with him.

I decided to make one last choice in our relationship and confess my feelings the rest was up to fate. I sent him an email that contained only the following quote:

"I know that you believe you understand what you think I said, but I'm not sure you realize that what you heard is not what I meant."

He called on his way home from work that evening.

I did not let my tongue hesitate because I was afraid my lips would find away to stay sealed, "I think I've fallen for you, I'm pretty sure you had my heart awhile ago, I'm just so scared."

His reply was softer than lavender dryer sheets, "I've been waiting to hear you say that. So much of what's happened between us is because you didn't want this and so I put my walls up."

"You have to believe me, I want to try. I think I may leave town for the month of December, and I want to see you before I go."

He was willing to see me, and he was willing to give us a try. We made plans to see each other and right then I knew I was going to drastically change my course of action and do what I needed to do to give us a fighting chance.

Just before I stepped out of the house to head to Savannah's Dad's I went on the hunt for my cross pendant necklace and slipped it around my neck. I picked up a bottle of Beaujolais Nouveau for me and pumpkin pie for him. When I got to the front door I realized I had no key. I stood staring at the locked door attempting whether or not I should bust open the screen to get inside.

Then I glanced around the neighborhood (as if anyone really cared) and lifted the mat. Sure enough, my key was still there. That was almost worse. I pathetically picked it up and unlocked the door. I was immediately mowed over by Savannah who, up until now, had been the reason I kept coming back time and time again. But this time I was here for her Dad.

He came home shortly after and ordered in Chinese food. The evening was nothing short of perfect.

We talked about his day at work and politics and how in the event of a Great Depression he would pack us up a fifth wheel trailer. We could drive up to my parent's house and live on their land and we laughed over nonsense and shared inconsequential chatter. I watched as he played with the girls. He was leaning against the counter in the kitchen, his work shirt was unbuttoned and un-tucked and as usual I found him incredibly sexy. I got up from the couch and stood in front of him, taking in the way his white under shirt hung on his stomach muscles.

"Do you mind if I do a test?" I asked.

"Not at all. What is it?"

I explained the test and as he extended his palm upright he began to look nervous. I unhooked my cross pendant from around my neck and then dangled it over his palm, it shook side to side and then stopped. He did the test to himself with the same result. Then he took my palm and did the test to me, and then I did it to myself just to be certain. We were both having one child, a boy.

He looked up from my open palm. His blue eyes had never been as piercing as he said, "I guess we should get started." And then he gave me a grin that made me melt, followed by a smirk that made me laugh.

We slurped down egg drop soup and crunchy wontons and then found a space in between Rio and Savannah to lay tight together, my fortune cookie from months before was coming true.

His hands were always my favorite. From the moment I first watched him shift the gears in the Jeep, while singing way off key to Kenny Rogers and Led Zeppelin. He reached for the remote and clicked on the movie and just as he began to pull the blanket over the top of us I watched his hand slowly slide down the curve of my waist and his fingers slip under the side of my panty.

The tips of his fingers might as well have been doused in kerosene because the minute he touched me it was like a spark lit and my whole body was on fire. The sounds coming from the television became a jumbled mess as he slowly pulled my spaghetti tank and bra-strap down my shoulder, his hands reached around to my chest as he pressed his lips to my back.

I didn't just crave him like I had in the past; I wanted him. I wanted every ounce of who he was, even the part I was convinced was brain damaged. Neither of us held anything back.

A Mercedes, a Jeep and a trailer on my parent's property, oil and water, passion and hard work, loyalty and lust, a heck of team, married but not really, best friends who want to kill each other. Never before had clearly confused felt so right.

But it didn't last long enough.

I knew that one night of perfection wouldn't take us as far as the months of passion had. If anything it worsened the situation, because now we shared hope for a future.

We both knew we still needed to talk, especially in light of the fact that I was debating whether to stay in San Diego for the remainder of the holidays. But rather than broaching the topic of the real issues, I decided to revel in the excitement of being clearly confused a bit longer. I figured it was okay to procrastinate on the conversation so long as I got my feelings down on paper. So instead of talking to him, I wrote him a letter. One I didn't intend to give him if things panned out. I left it in my car.

When his text came through a few days later, reality didn't change the fact that I wanted to crawl under a rock, all it said was:

We should talk.

If I had a time capsule, I would have gone back in time to the moment when we first made love, because back then that's what it was. At that time my heart wasn't with him, and he knew it. If I could have gone back I would have left less up to me and more up to fate.

I called him. He asked me to stay quiet while he spoke…

He said he had wanted me to fall in love with him and I wouldn't. (But then I did.)

He said he can't believe my heart is suddenly in this and he's not sure his is now. (I shared his doubts.)

He said he cared too much to hurt me. (My guilty conscience fought myself every day.)

He told me he wanted more for so long, but wonders if we'd kill each other now. (I know I sabotaged us and created that fear.)

He said he cried on his way home, because he loves me. (I cried too because I realized I couldn't change the fact that I was deeply and emotionally attached to him.)

He said what we did to each other wasn't fair;
and that the distance, my trip to Georgetown for
the holidays, would be good for both of us to clear
our heads. (I agreed because more than anything
I needed distance for clarity.)

He said that if the stars were aligned when I got
back to San Diego, then we could give it a go, one
hundred and ten percent, for real, exclusively.

I told him I loved him.

He said he knew that and it killed him. He told me to leave town, he couldn't do it anymore and he wanted to be alone.

I couldn't bring myself to give him the letter I kept tucked in the car for over a week.

THE LETTER

December was only a few days away and I felt like I was on a self destructive path. I knew there was only one place I could truly clear my head and get my arms around my life. I knew Savannah's Dad was right, staying in San Diego would cheat us both. There was only one place I could finish writing the final chapter for the book. The pen truly is mightier than the sword and I knew my own handwriting would be hard to swallow. There was only one place I could gain clarity and only one place that I would feel safe reading through a year's worth of journals, Georgetown.

So I packed up the car, the cat and the dog and headed north on Interstate 5. As I sat at a gas station in Castaic waiting to hear the gas pump shut off, when I spotted the letter I'd tucked in the side pocket of the driver's seat.

Dear Savannah's Dad,

I spent the night thinking and not thinking about you and I.

I wonder if I could go back in time and erase my fear…or stop my heart from being with someone else a little sooner, where would we be today?

I'm guilty too. I put you first as a friend and a lover, but never as my man.

Part of me hopes I get back to San Diego and enough time has passed and both of us realize it's what we want, because maybe then we'll have a fighting chance.

And part of me is terrified that we'll go our separate ways. Just know you're the last thing I think about before I go to sleep, and the first when I wake up, followed immediately by, what-if…I hate that somewhere along the way you got your fingertips around my heart. If it's what you wanted, you got it. Pride aside, I've fallen for you.

It was easier to be in denial and stay in love with a man that wasn't available than be in love with the man who was standing right there.

I'll always regret that because I do love you.

Michaela

I only wish I could have figured that out sooner, because at that moment clearly confused didn't feel so right anymore.

THE LIST

My new game plan was to spend a month living with Mom and Dad. I needed to gain clarity and I didn't want to be alone for the holidays.

In the few days before I left I managed to see all my friends, except "Mister Disappointment," who was frequently living up to his name. I even saw Savannah's Dad for a quick goodbye hug. I accepted that I was not running away, I was simply choosing to take time for me, to clear my head and evaluate all the experiences I'd had over the prior year.

As I made the first hairpin curve down into the Auburn ravine I took a deep breath. It was golden hour as I reached my parents street, and as I approached the pond I stopped the car in the middle of the road to take a photo.

Not much had changed since the first time I kicked up the driveway crammed in the back of the Jeep with my brothers at twelve years old except to say my ride was a lot nicer. I programmed the pre-set radio stations in my trusty Benz and clicked to 105.1 KNCI. Taylor Swift was singing "Love Story."

The fraction of a girl who rode down the escalator with tears in her eyes almost exactly a year before was gone, and the young lady who packed her bags and left for college in 1997 had come home for the holidays, as if it were the first time since I'd left.

My Uggs crunched the pine needles as I stepped out into the chilly winter air. I pulled my Northface fleece a little tighter to my chest and dug around in my pocket for the list. The smell of the pine and madrone was overwhelming and I actually took a sigh of relief. It was either that or the light mountain air had stolen my breath. I unfolded the list I'd kept for well over a year and read the items one by one.

Will dust off my knees when I fall and kiss the owie to make it better

Let me wear his shirt (and say I look good in it)

Someone who eats the pizza, so I can eat the crust

A guys guy who walks me to the dance floor and leads me in the dance, even if he's a terrible dancer

Will make sure I have a candle on my birthday, because the wish is most important

A travel buddy who is willing to see the world with me, because I want to see it all

Will stand up for me, as his partner

Says "I love you" encompassing passion, trust and friendship

Will never hurt me —physically or otherwise, and understands the power of an apology

TEETERING ON DISASTER

*Can appreciate a Ferrari, but knows how to drive
an old rusty Jeep*

*Loves my dog and loves country music, because at
the bottom of my heart, I'm a country girl*

I'd been at the house unpacking; when I heard Dad and Mom come in the back door. I paused to peek my head around the corner as I heard Dad yell, "Hey Sis, is it really you? Are you here to bless us with your presence?"

And to that we all started cackling.

"JEEZ Dad, I just went through a divorce what makes you think I have money to buy you presents!"

WRITE OFF DAY DECEMBER 31, 2008 (CLARITY CONFIRMED)

By the end of December I'd completely dove into life with my family. We went snow-wheelin, we chopped down our own Charlie Brown Christmas tree (but this time all seven feet of it fit inside the house), we baked cookies and sucked down spike Orange Julius.

As the hours and days ticked by during the festive month of December, I thought about all the things I'd done over the last year, all the people I'd met; those who loved me and added value to my life. I wondered how through all the difficult times I managed to stand back up and how I managed to stay on the course, even though it was a bumpy dirt road.

I realized it wasn't a course that I had to follow, but a journey that I created as I went along. Years before sitting in a trailer, on a small piece of land in Georgetown as just a young woman, I'd been taught how to rock crawl when the road got rough. Those skills brought me down the bumpy road stronger than ever before.

Though I was surrounded by family I had a lot of time to think back on the relationships I'd created and grown and those that I'd lost in the past year. One afternoon amidst a snowstorm in the middle of December an email reply finally came through from "Mister Disappointment." I'd asked him to read his "chapter" and to please share his thoughts on what had caused him to run so many months before:

> From: Mister Disappointment
> To: Michaela
> Subject: RE: Clearly Confused
>
> *I deleted your original email, so I'll do my best.*
>
> *First of all, the chapter should be Dr. Disappointment—I have a PhD in making people feel like shit J.*
>
> *Basically, I was thinking "wow, this girl is coming on fast!" Lots of calls, a litany of emails, etc. Who knows, maybe I wasn't ready to date either, but that's how I felt.*
>
> *After awhile it just made you sound very insecure, which only expedited my departure. Knowing you now—I don't think that's completely true...but I will say you don't need to constantly tell people how great you are. We know you're great...*

TEETERING ON DISASTER

I hope this helps…you said to brutally honest.

Dr. Disappointment

From: Michaela
To: Mister Disappointment
Subject: Re: Clearly Confused

*Makes sense, the burning question though is:
Why the push/pull? Why didn't you let me walk
away completely?*

*Post Script: That's funny because 1. I was inse-
cure 2. I felt like a complete failure :-)*

*Sincerely,
Greatness. ;)*

From: Mister Disappointment
To! Michaela
Subject: RE: Clearly Confused

*Oh, whoops! I was afraid if I blew you off you'd
never talk to me again—basically you're too
interesting to not have in my life…*

You're not a failure…not even close.

*Regards,
Sadness Messiah*

For once I read one of his emails with eyes wide open. He was being brutal with me because he was upset. I spoke to Sarita that day and she wholeheartedly agreed that his angry response was only because he was wounded. Clarity was confirmed, "Operation Shovel Dirt" aborted.

I realized emailing him back would only hurt him further. So I waited a few days and when I finally responded I sent a loving note. I had no regrets for our past, and I secretly still hoped for a future. But I was finally standing completely on my own two feet, walking one hundred percent for me. The vision in my head was clear and glistening like golden hour across the pond. Everything was exactly as it was meant to be.

A few days after that I received an email that said Savannah's Dad had added me as a friend on Facebook. I couldn't help but laugh when I accepted the request. I also couldn't help but tear up a little when a few days later the text photo came through with a picture of Savannah that said:

Hello Mommy, I miss you

And even though "Mister Disappointment" still silently sailed the tide with me and his spark lighted my heart; and even though Savannah's Dad provided my mind the comfort it needed to feel secure again, it wasn't either of them who taught me how to stand when I wanted to run. It wasn't any man at all.

It was a photo text message of Savannah and what she said without saying. When you ride on faith you can fall apart, shatter to pieces, you can teeter on disaster, or you can plunge right off. But you'll always be ok. By the end of my journey I had learned that:

SETTLING for a short while is not bad, as long as you still follow your dreams, BOUNDARIES and ENTITLEMENT are basic fundamentals to creating inner strength, EXPECTATIONS should be set, but it's only when you let them go that they are met, DISAPPOINTMENT is the only way to see value in your blessings, COURAGE is being able to spend some time at rock bottom, FRIENDSHIP is everywhere but only found when you quit looking for it, STRENGTH can not be measured by anything less than your ability to stand up when you fall regardless of how long it takes you to get back on your feet, JUDGMENT is necessary for one person to realize their own faults, FORGIVENESS is the gift we are afforded to share grace with one another, CLOSURE can only be created by the one needing it, otherwise it's not closure at all, CIRCUMSTANCE is fate and having faith when the direction of the road isn't clear, CONFUSION is required to gain a better understanding of the depths of your soul because sometimes your mind and your heart disagree, LOVE allows the heart ease from the greatest of all pains, TRUST is deserved and earned and should be considered a reward, CLARITY comes when all of those pieces arrive together in synchronistic harmony.

If not, there's always Write Off Day...so then there's that.

About the Author

Michaela Renee Johnson is a licensed psychotherapist, freelancer writer for the Mountain Democrat (the oldest publication in California), public speaker, small business owner and award winning published author. She lives in Northern California with her husband and son, and a homestead full of animals. She enjoys traveling and has visited 19 countries; she loves the ocean and everything in it. She rarely finds herself without an activity whether it be hiking, yoga, tinkering the garden, golfing, reading or spending time outside. In her simplest she loves poetic quotes and all things metaphysical.

Cover Design & Photography: Ryche Guerrero
printscharming.com
Author Photo: ©2017, Stephanie Sutherlin